Y U N H E E   M I N

YUNHEE MIN

ESSAYS BY DANIEL MENDEL-BLACK AND JAN TUMLIR

SUSANNE VIELMETTER LOS ANGELES PROJECTS

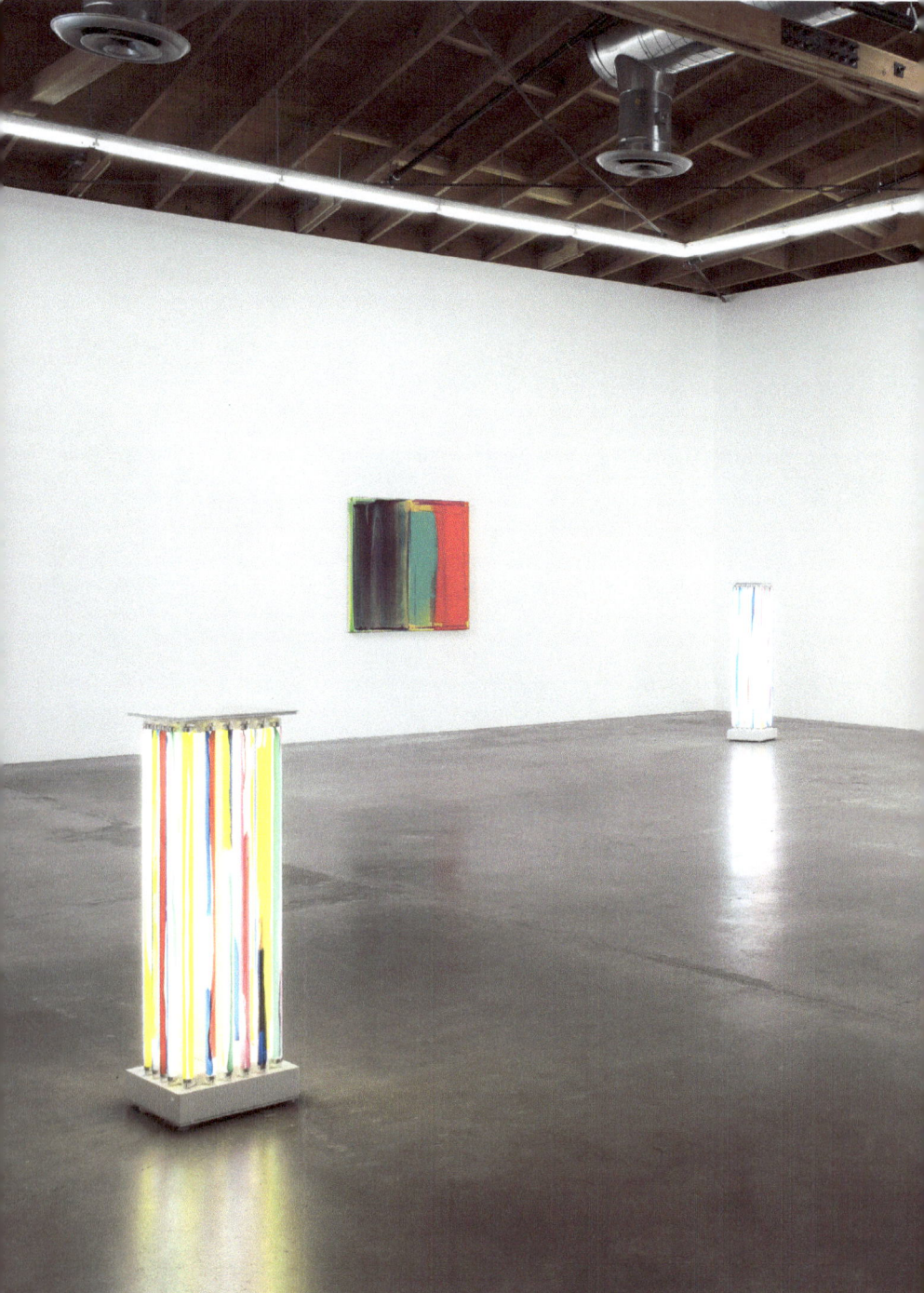

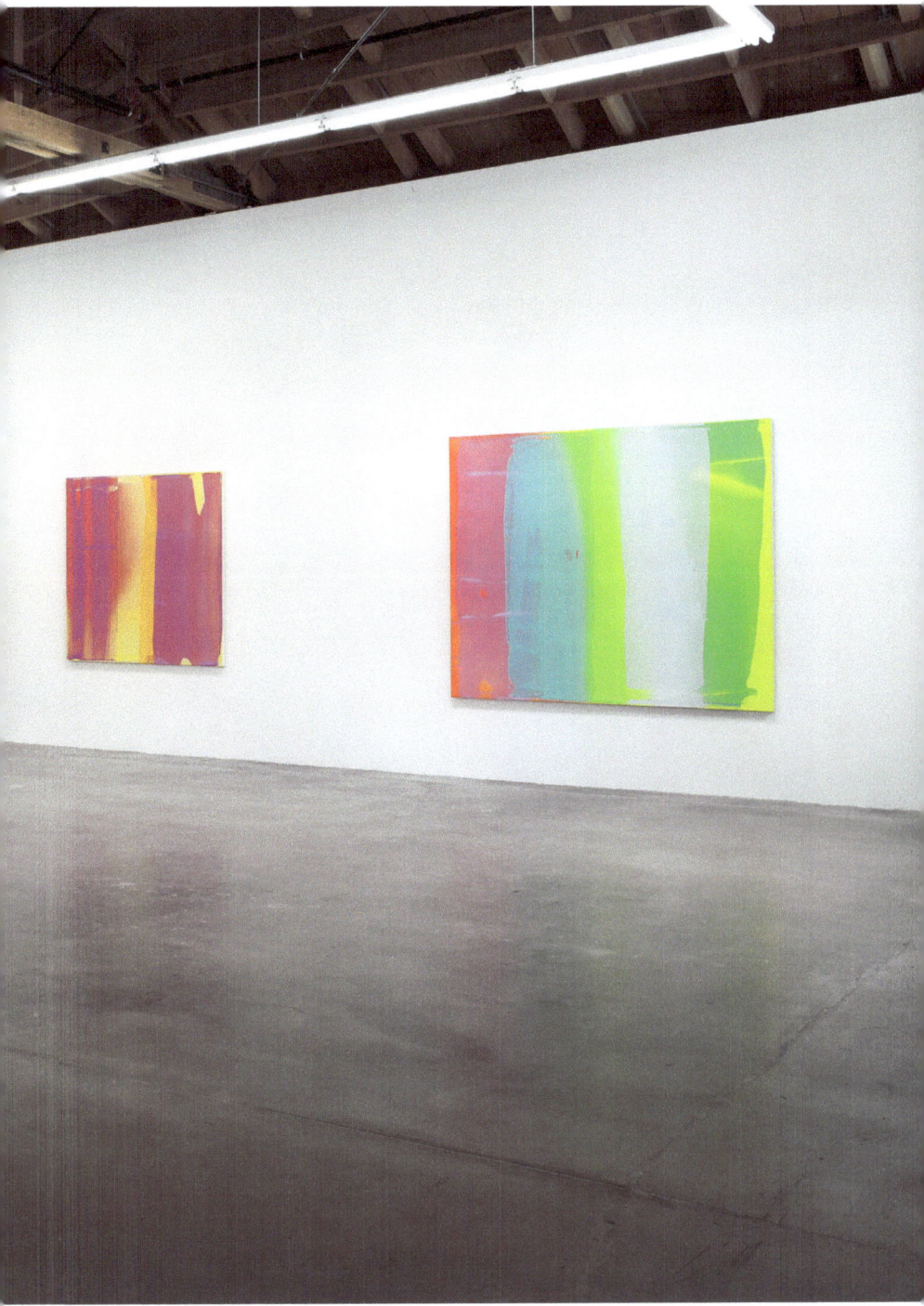

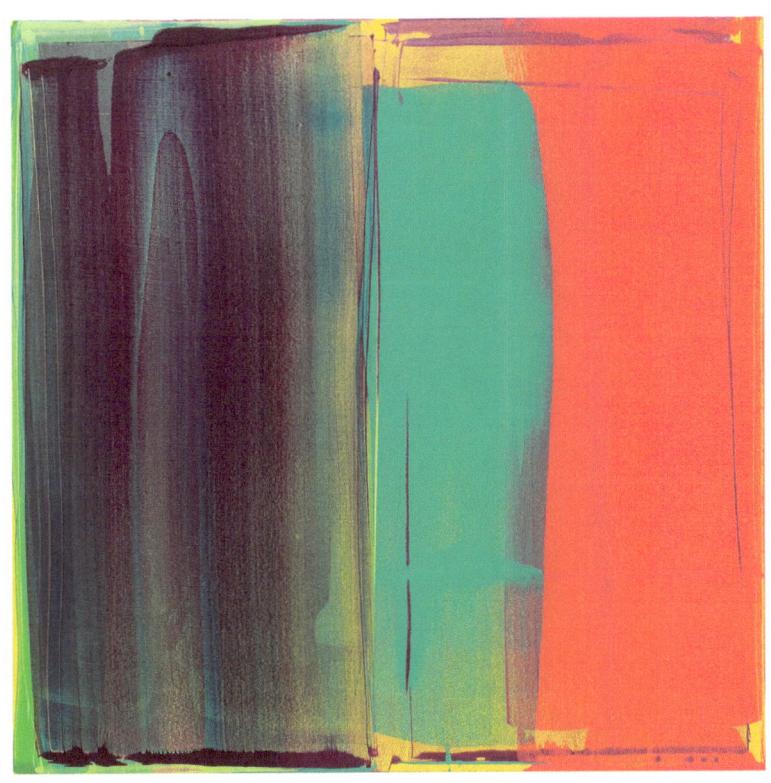

Eternal Summer
Daniel Mendel-Black

A distinctive, penetrating, compressed light is generated from the modulated pressure of Yunhee Min's application of paint on her canvas surface—the kind of vibrant color that is synonymous with heat. In the past, the more common terms of choice to describe a painter's presence in the work were "gesture" or "mark making," neither of which, however, seems in her case, like a particularly good fit. Cézanne's use of regular diagonal lines in his later landscapes comes to mind because of the way the delicacy of his palette and brushwork combined in the peculiar choice of color inspired by his lifetime spent in the south of France. Clyfford Still's heavy, crusty, flat, repetitive application of paint, on the other hand, could serve as a good counter-example to the way she approaches the canvas. In any case, Min's specific "touch" is what we are left with, literally how she lays on the paint, and the allusion to the exotic shimmer of the hot neon nights and sunny days of Southern California's eternal summer that is so strangely manifested in these paintings.

As anyone who has followed her work appreciates, Min is a colorist, and like any such painter, it quickly becomes clear that the most consistently rewarding approach is to let the color do as much of the hard work as possible—to allow for the unex- pected result of the chance occurrence of paint build-up, puddling, mingling, and all the myriad other potential surprises wet medium and pigment can offer. Anything the artist can do to get out of the way of the end result, so the ethos goes, will only garner a better outcome. Consequently, there is a desire to confuse the situation as little as possible with the presence of the hand, which has the unfortunate tendency, as soon as it is spotted, to get psychologized, and to keep such an interference at bay as long as possible, always at a healthy remove, through the use of some distancing mechanism or other, such as a stick, weighted brush, or squeegee. To that end, anything goes, that is, anything short of the total physical remove from the activity of making the painting, because there is also the equally significant recogni- tion among such painters that they are first and foremost lifelong students of light and color, and as the old saw goes, the only way to learn is by doing. Kandinsky, for example, liked to use the term "materialist" to describe his method, not in the ideological and hence judgmental sense, but rather as a way of describing a picture that could only get discovered through the manipulation of the visceral, worldly physicality of paint.

Min's path to the present body of work was indirect. Like a number of paint- ers from her generation, early on she was drawn to the brand of rationale offered by conceptual practices, the kind of consideration, at least where painting was concerned, primarily characterized by objectification. Whether in Daniel Buren, or Sol LeWitt, let's say, the strategy was often to literalize the medium, to relocate it in the all-around space of architecture, for instance, and redirect the discussion from that of the lyrical space of the picture plane to the painting as a structure in the world. Objectification was the great insight of the Enlightenment and there would, in fact, be no science as we know it today without the kind of cold, hard scrutiny symbolized by the butterfly pinned to a board and framed on a wall. For a while at the end of the last century, if the artist wanted to seem smart about painting or, conversely, if he or she wished to poke fun, the most common way to do so was to re-conceive the medium as an analytical object of study and reflection. Either way, by disallowing a broader discussion, such a gesture, even if it opened up a semiotic field of discussion, as was sometimes the case, proved reductive in other significant regards. Min's earlier work, inspired by that period is, not surprisingly, trapezoidal and leans sculpturally at an angle rather than maintaining the verticality necessary for the painting surface to exist unencumbered.

Often, when the space of abstraction is described, some of the more common terms of choice are: "oceanic," "atmospheric," even "nebular." Especially where the light touch is concerned, Turner is the undisputed champion. It is not simply that his favorite subjects are in the roiling sea, the haze of the marine layer, the approaching storm, etc.; his last ghostly works, at least among certain painters, are considered some of his best. The uncertainty over whether they were ever actually completed or are only the most meager initial sketches of under-painting doesn't seem to matter. The marks are no less deliberate for their seeming weightlessness, as if they were bleached out like over-exposed photographs taken on a bright day. If only barely visible, the presence of their subject is no less felt. By contrast, it is difficult to talk about a term like "touch" in a correspondingly spatial Morris Louis curtain painting because it is clear from the outset that the washes of color were poured from a location outside the painting. The light produced is enveloping, as if we are looking up at the sun from under a parachute.

With her latest abstractions Min arguably splits the difference between implied space and systematic application. No longer is the canvas a play on the architectural object. These are full-frontal works emphasizing the field, their shimmering transparent layers entirely concerned with painterly depth. Neither are they atmospheric in the soupy, moody way that a Turner can be, nor are they quite as insistently flowing and ethereal as a Louis. The pressure applied to the squeegee that allows for the paint to puddle more opaquely in certain places than in others to cause the modulated intensification or diffusion of color, or the stuttered up-and-down motion that creates a wavering, crackling ribbon-like effect of a buzzing light is a direct trace indicator of the artist's presence as she gently presses her implement up against the surface and gracefully (yet firmly) drags it vertically across the canvas. At the same time, the palpable softness of her applied force is reminiscent of the quality of lightness in Turner's late work when the color is pressed as thinly as possible; the receding veils are closer to the kind of systematic approach to layering in Louis.

The key difference is that Min's abstractions do not swell with breezy, cool air in the same way as the work of either of those painters. Not by a long-shot. There is nothing gray or cloudy in her pictures. They are not soothing or enveloping. There is no shady place to curl up. The atmosphere in her paintings is about as breath-able as the hot gas in a fluorescent light bulb. You might as well suck on the tailpipe of a running car. Her work is more accurately about an impenetrable, artificial, glowing, bright light—a searing incandescence that threatens to suck all the oxygen out of the room at the same time as it fries your retina. Yet, Min, is after a more complicated and nuanced experience. As forceful as these paintings are, because of their light touch they are also undeniably majestic and elegant. Attraction and repulsion work to mysterious effects. At the last moment before you feel as if you are about to become consumed by the light, she interrupts the laser-harsh bright-ness with the cooler, more soothing film of a less aggressive, softer color in much the same way you put on a pair of dark sunglasses when you go outside to protect your naked eyes from the extreme, burning, high-contrast brightness of the endless procession of clear sunny days here in Southern California.

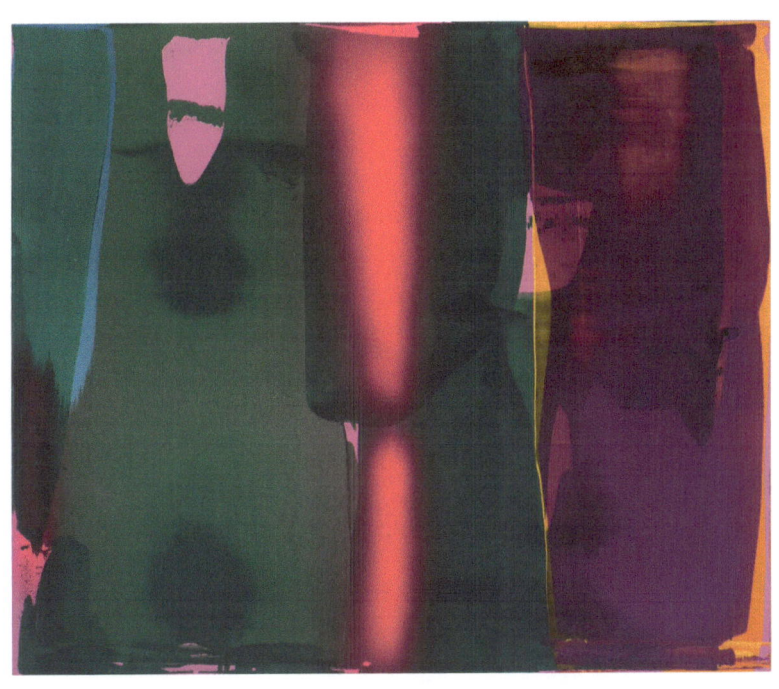

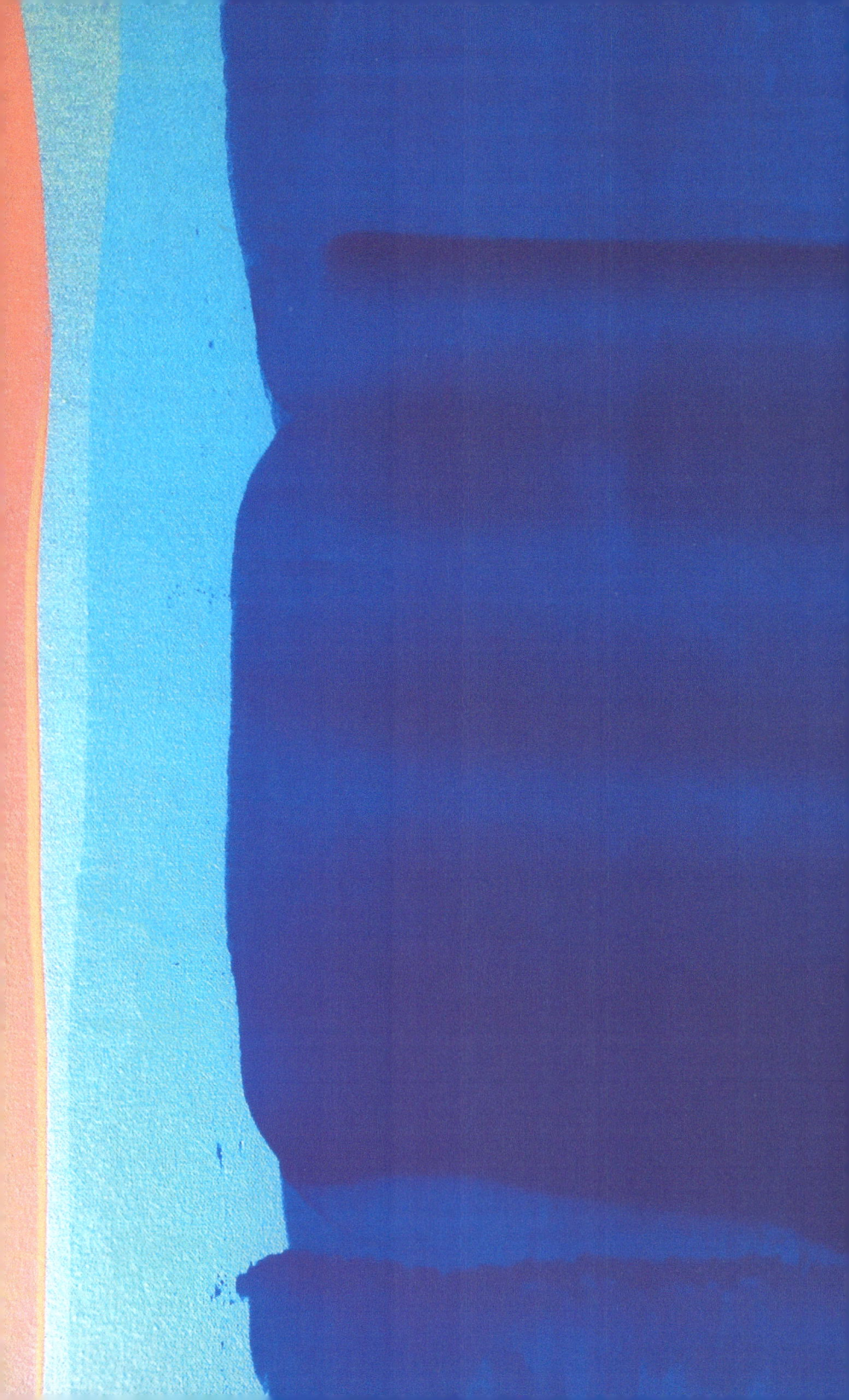

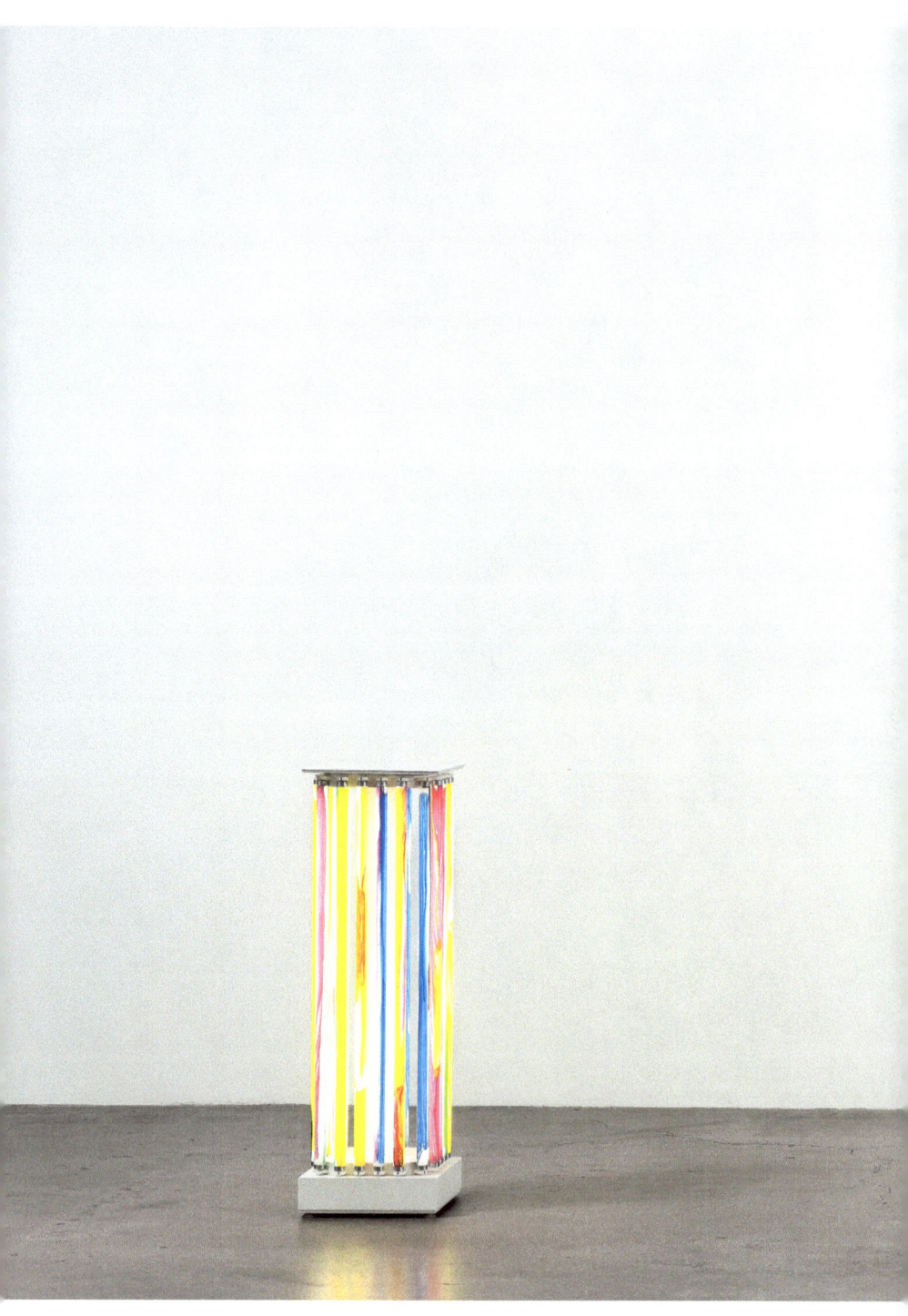

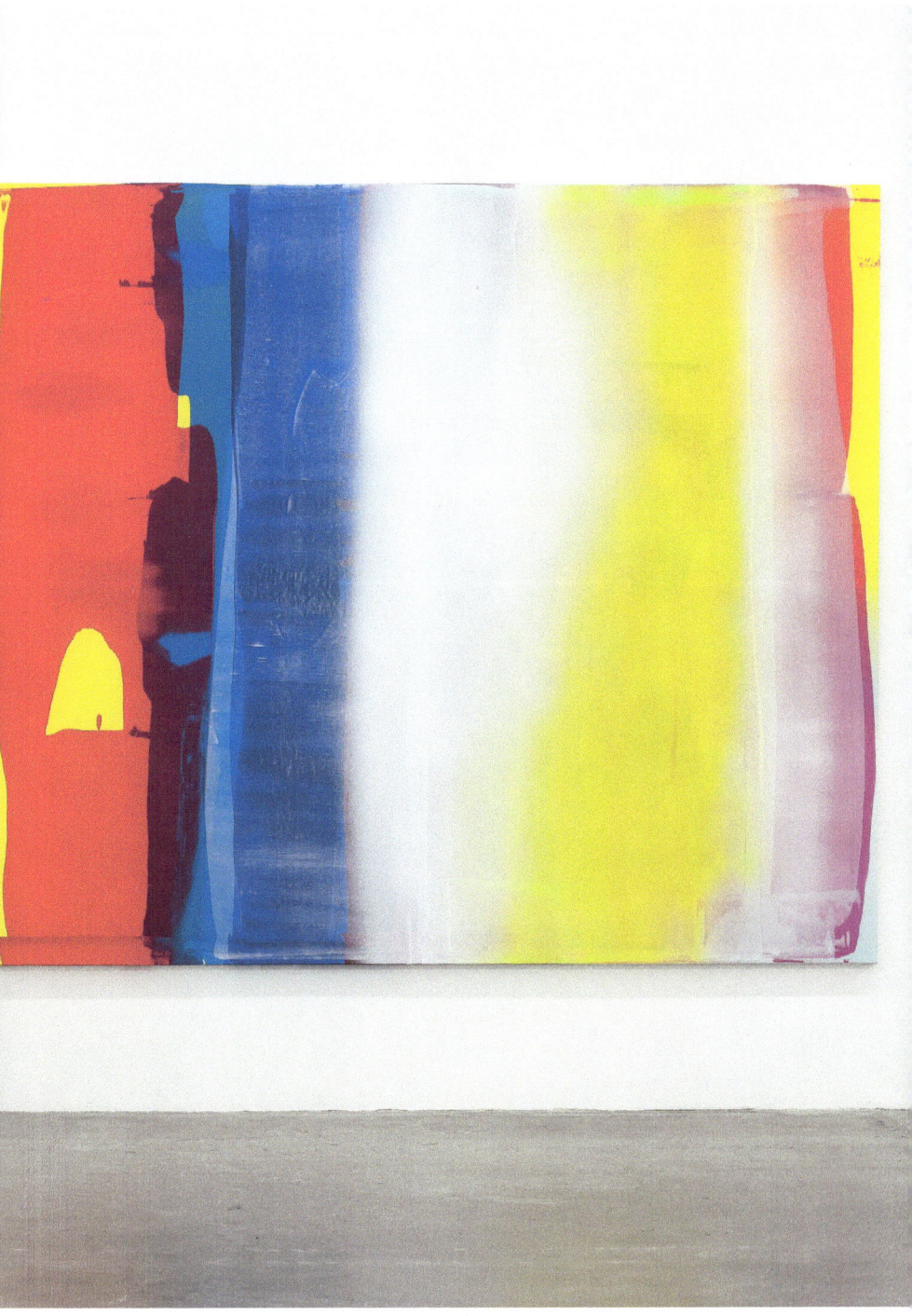

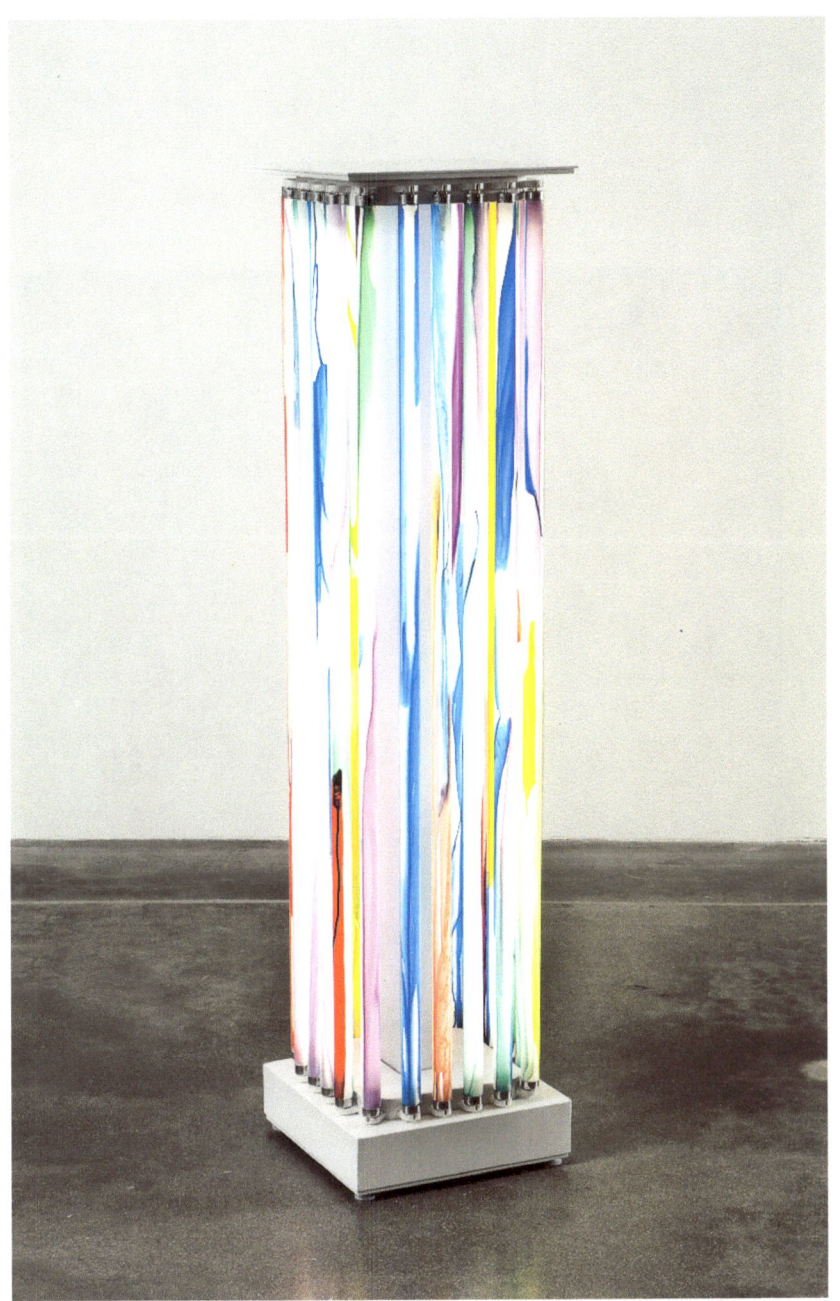

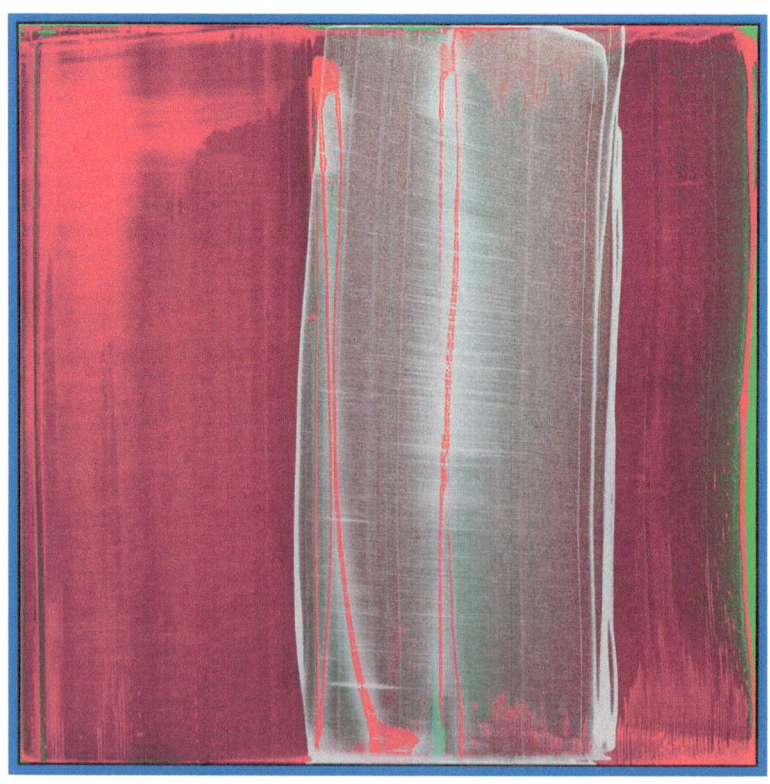

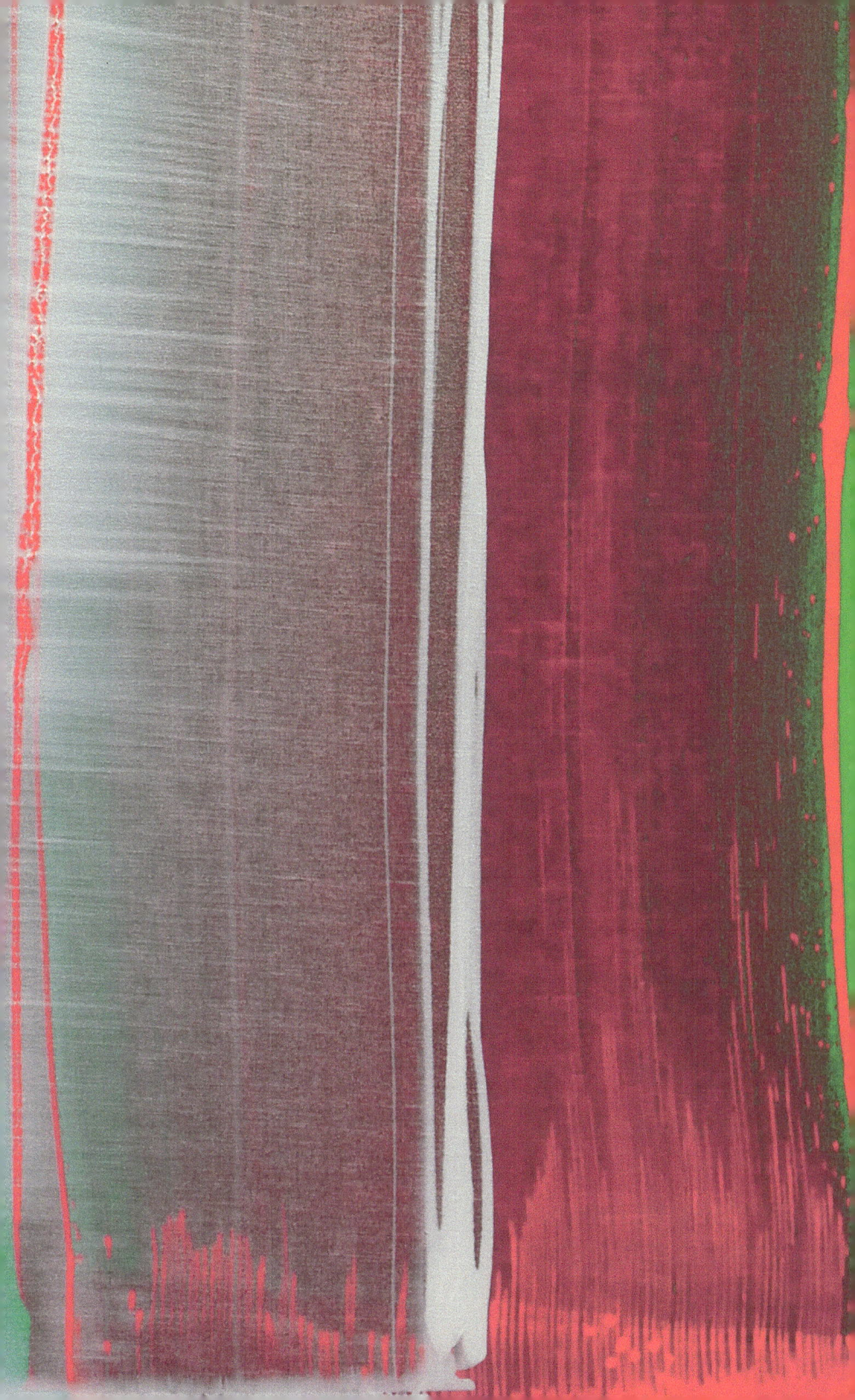

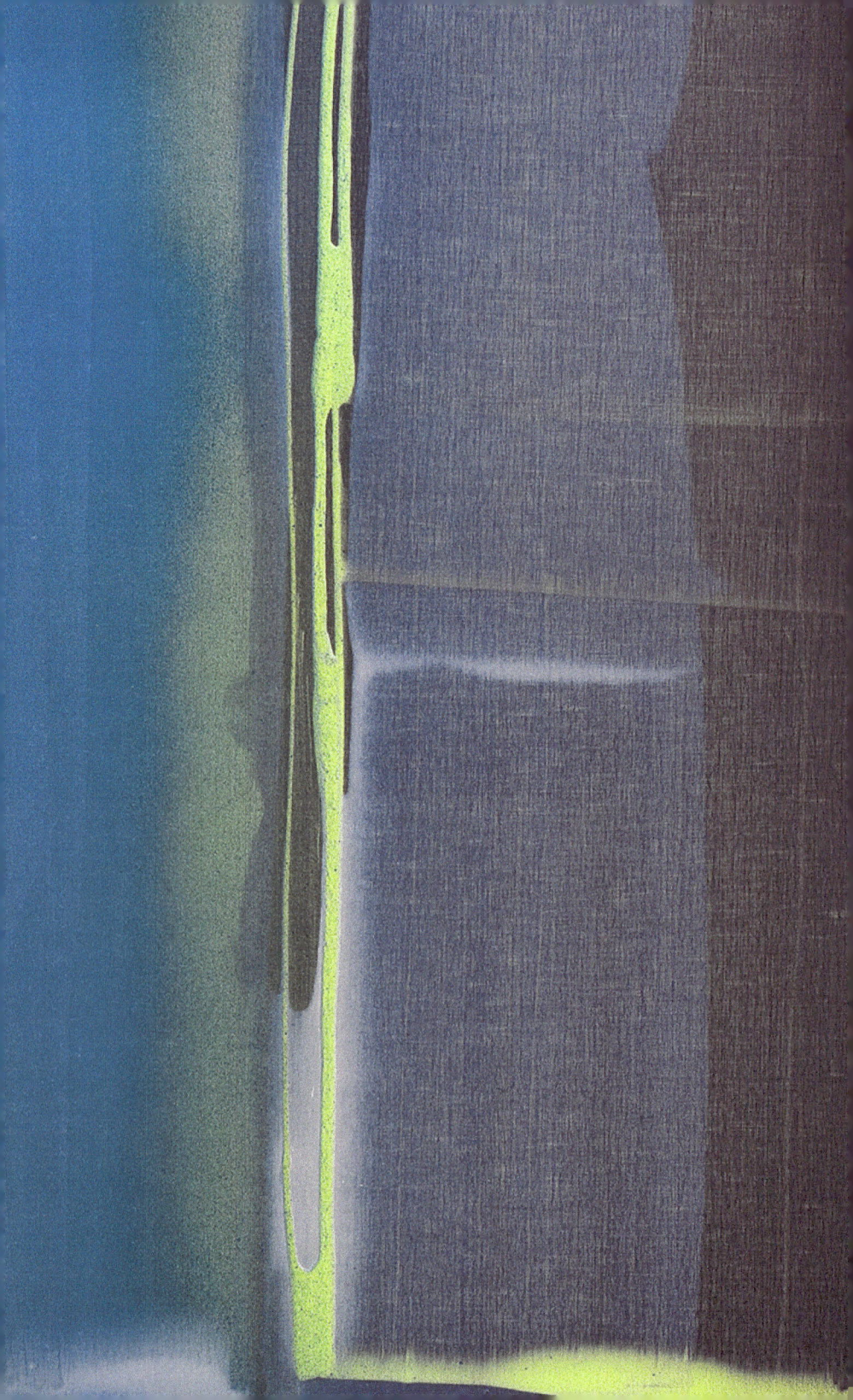

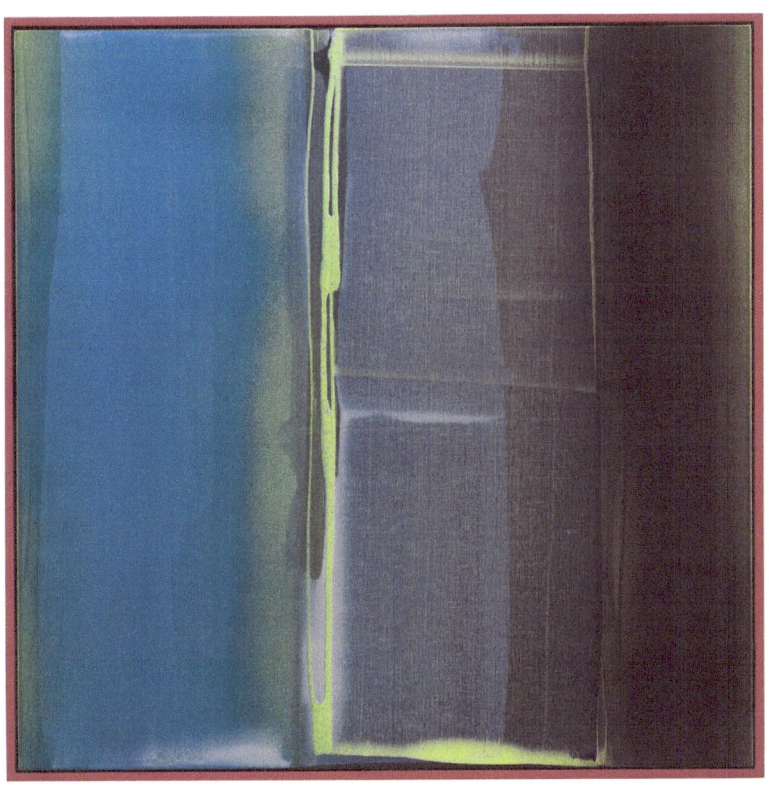

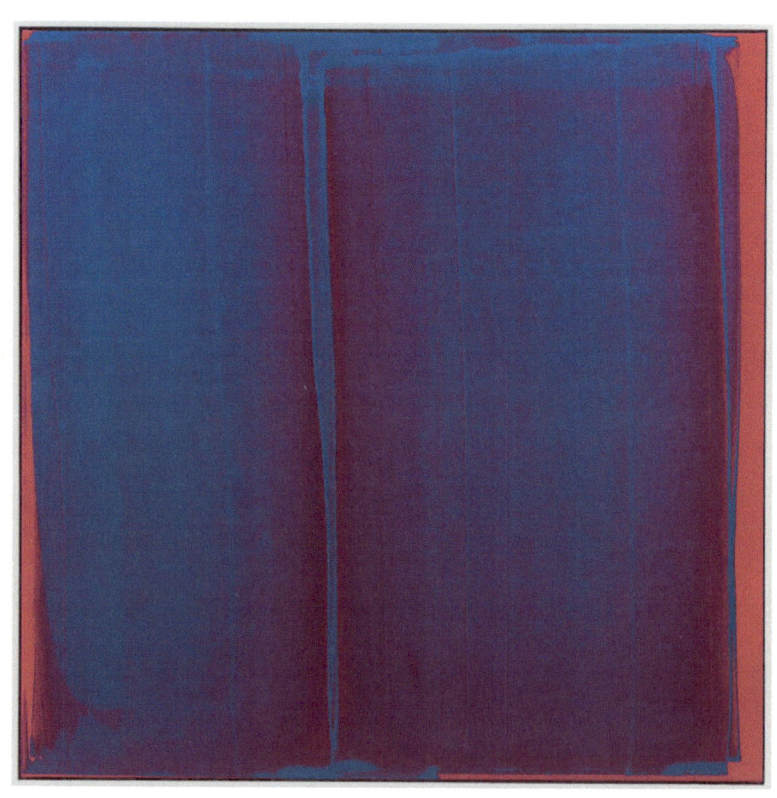

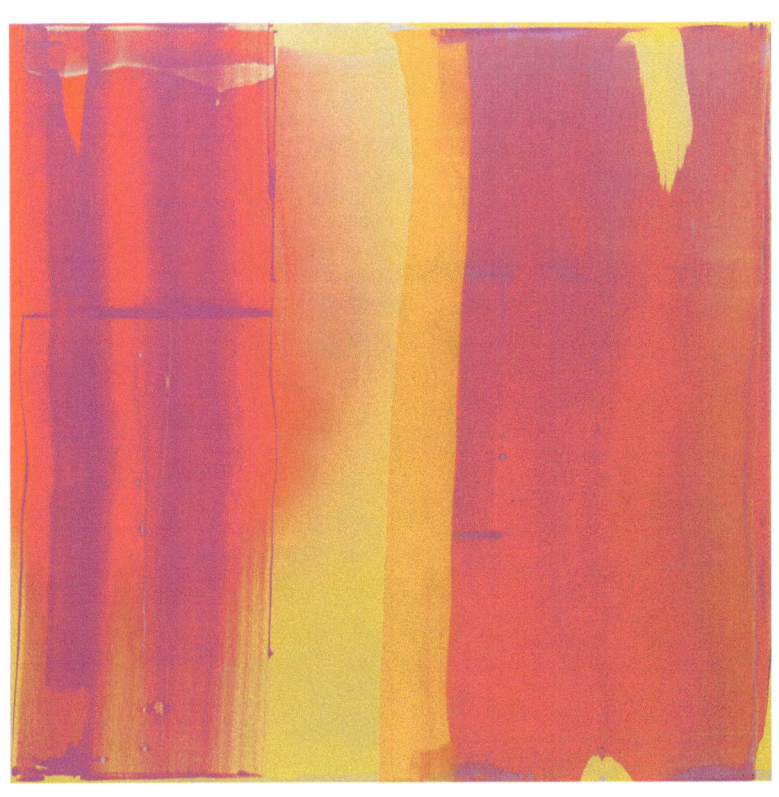

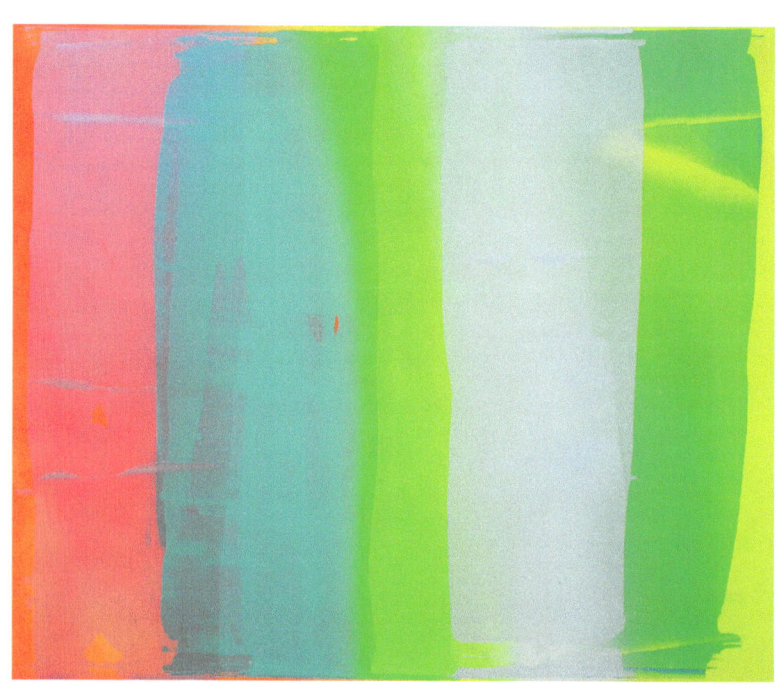

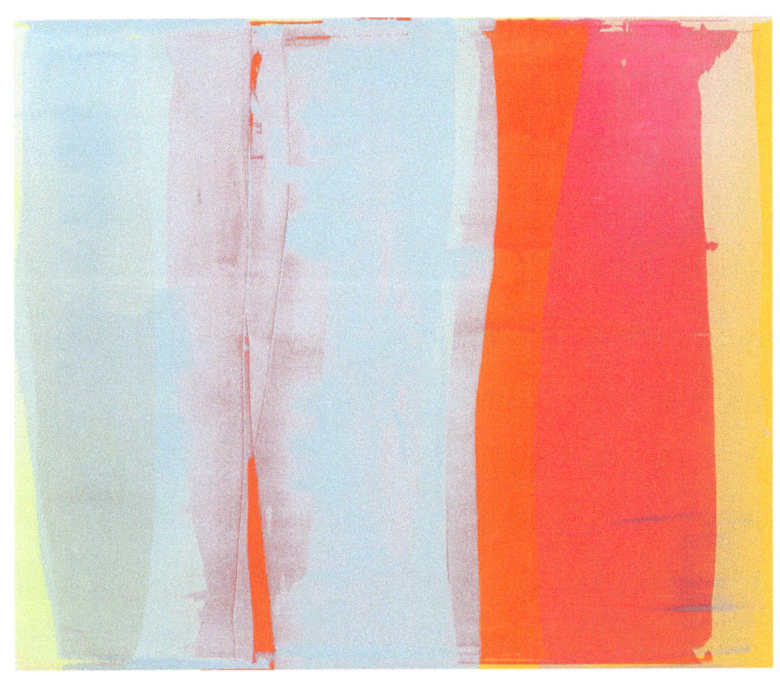

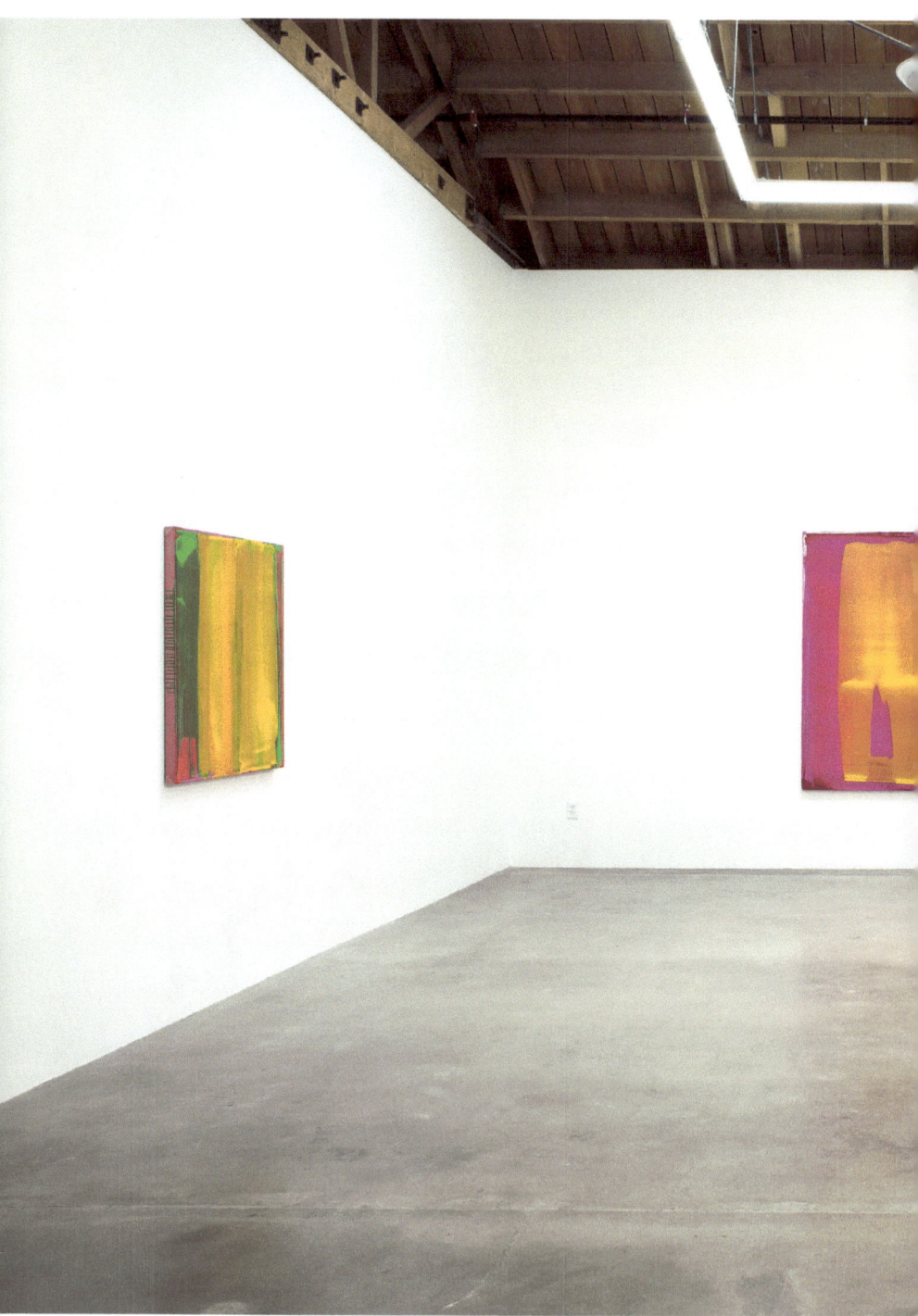

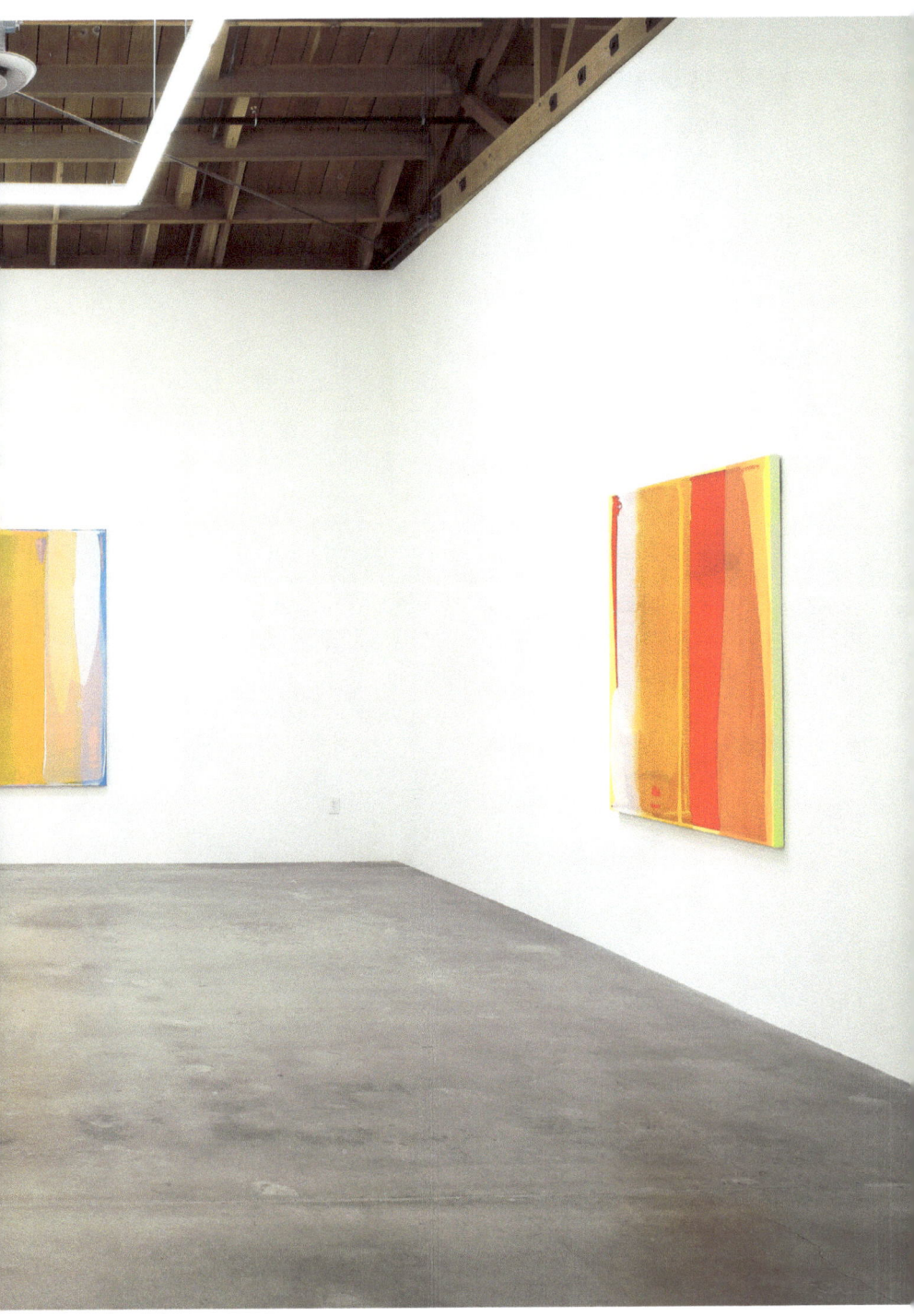

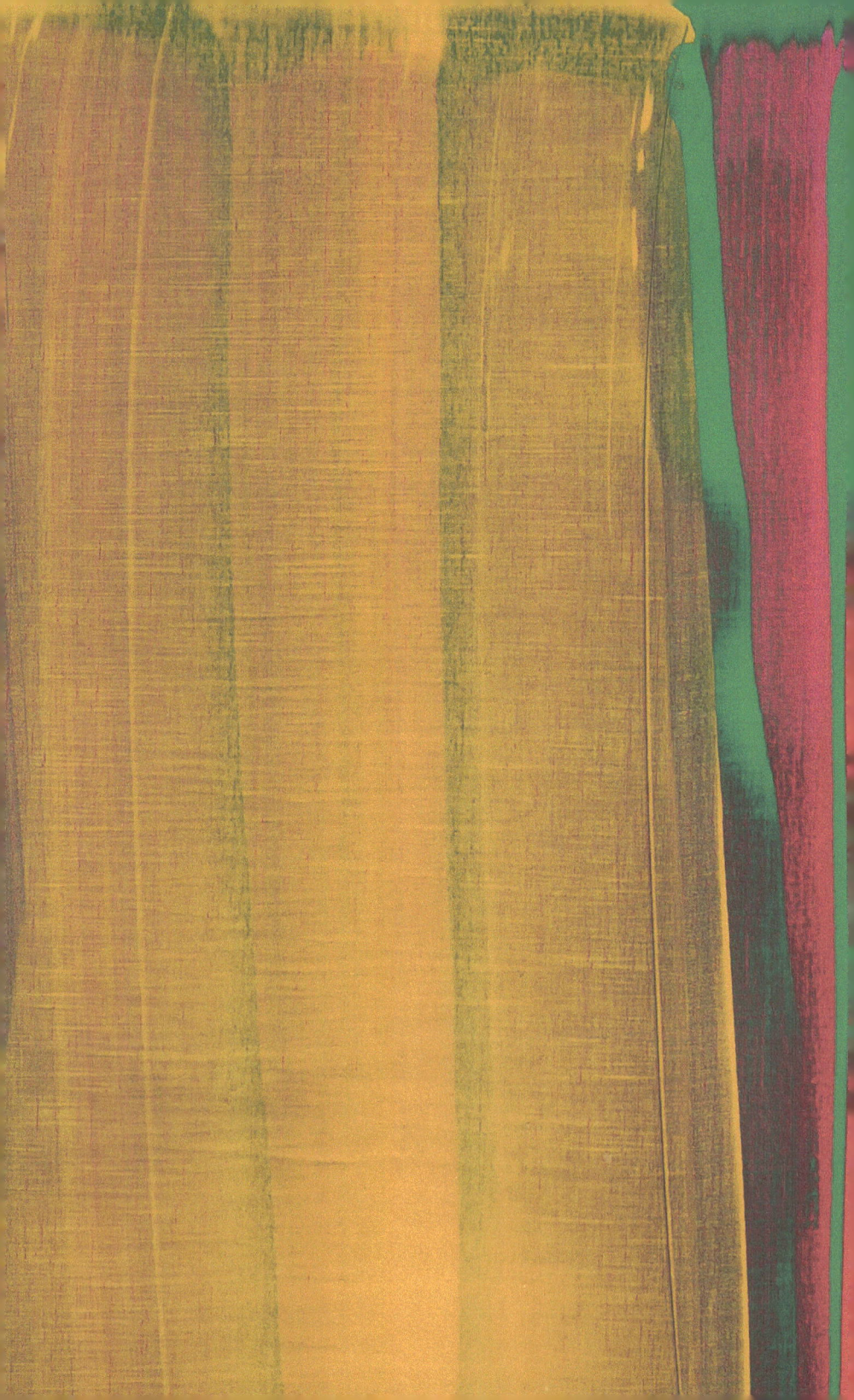

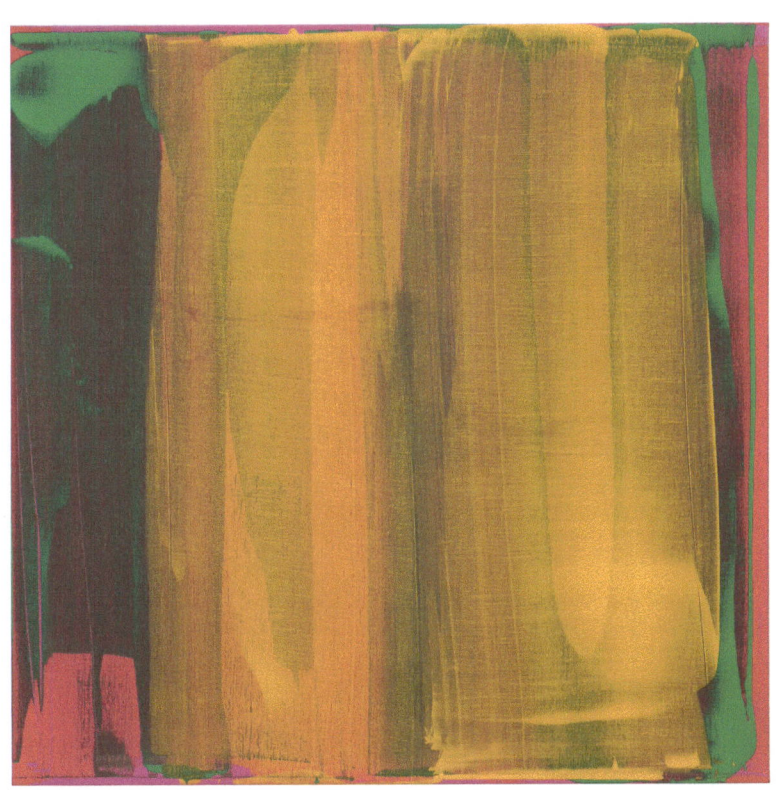

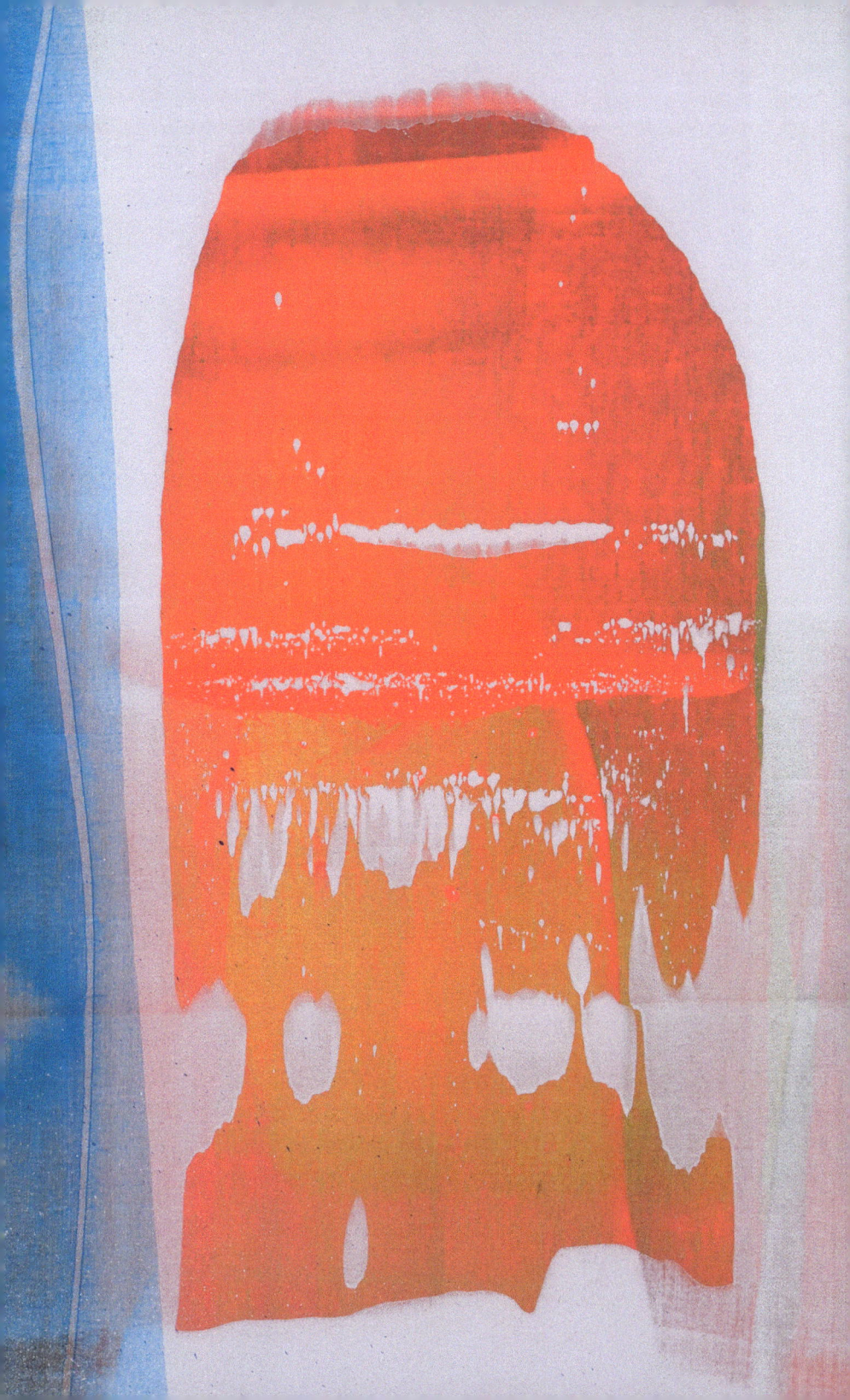

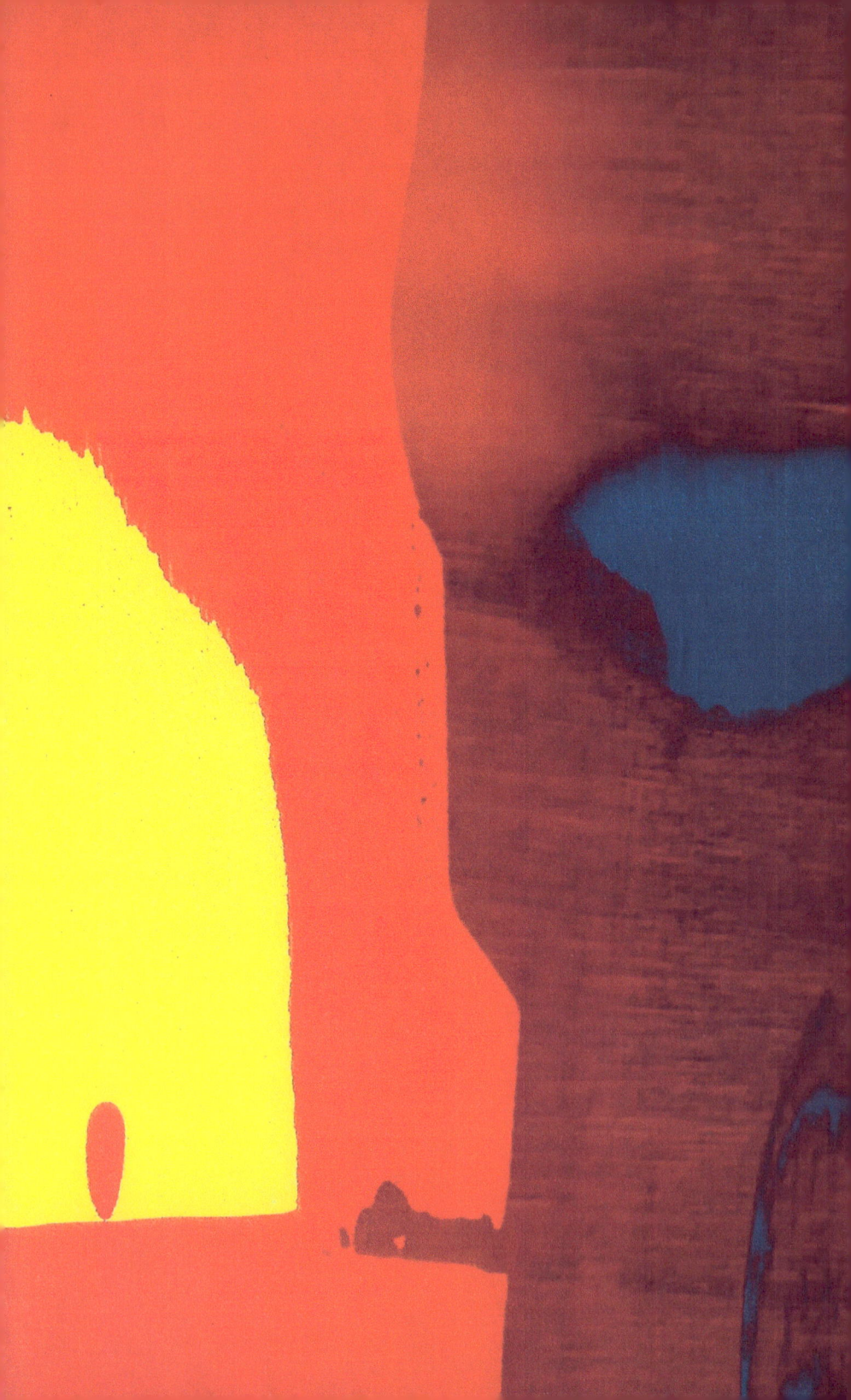

Yunhee Min: The Pass, The Band, The Color
Jan Tumlir

Yunhee Min is still largely known for her postminimalist cross-pollinations of painting and sculpture. That she pursued a degree in architecture some years after completing art school indicates a particular seriousness and ambition in this regard, as it is no longer enough to simply concretize painting's inherently virtual condition by extending it into actual space—that is, to transform painting, as the emblematic fetish of art, by way of its displacement from the eternal now of the white wall and into the contingent everyday world of things among things. Here, instead, painting would become a means of transforming space, whether as a structural element in the case of her painted and leaning wall sections, or as one of design and décor in the case of her tinted window treatments or dyed hanging (theatrical) curtain-like fabrics. In relation to these various transdisciplinary hybrids, her more recent output suggests a kind of retrenchment, for this consists of more or less conventional paintings, unobtrusively proportioned and scaled, and once more wall-hung and free-floating. Moreover, these paintings no longer bear just one evenly applied color but many, gesturally composed and boasting a wide range of finely tuned internal relations. Relations of parts, of discrete but interacting formal elements, invite us to approach the work as a world unto itself and to become absorbed in that world in a way that the work that is "all of one part," in the language of Donald Judd, categorically disallows. The un-composed and non-relational not-paintings and not-sculptures that Judd favored are left empty inside, so as to be filled in a spontaneous, aleatory manner with the real and existing conditions of life outside. Much the same could be said for Min's earlier works, which also automatically register the presence of all the persons, places and things that constitute their environment, but in these newer ones, what matters most is what is intentionally put inside the framing edge.

The former materialist equation of Minimalism, and by extension Constructivism, is upended by an absolute insistence on painting as a zone of perceptual concentration and subjective investment. However abstract, the work holds its place on the wall as a window of sorts onto outlying worlds, and a moveable plane. In its transportability, painting relates to the studio and gallery as transitional spaces, successive stops en route to the domestic interior as its final destination. There it can exercise to the fullest extent its prerogative to exist in and among us, in the midst of our most intimate day-to-day routines, while simultaneously claiming a state of exception, never fully belonging, always pointing somewhere beyond. Certainly Min's new paintings are primed to do just this: they flicker suggestively between objective flatness and pictorial depth, an intractable surface upon which layers of pigment have collected one atop another in a seemingly endless oceanic recession. Her meticulous technique recalls the exertions of the Washington School of Color Field painters to avoid any trace of material buildup on the canvas while nevertheless loading it with visual incident. Here, too, we are left stranded on the unsteady threshold that separates things from pictures, and hence also from memories, dreams, fantasies and hallucinations.

In Min's work, paint is poured onto stretched canvases placed face-up on the artist's worktable and then swiped across their length with squeegees in thick bands. The width of this mark-making implement is to an extent predetermined in relation to the overall surface area to allow for just one or several passes to sit side by side and occasionally comingle. In their general structure these works are resoundingly simple, almost rote, yet all kinds of painterly incidents accrue in the process. Changes in the pressure of the paint's application, its inherent density or thinness, the tautness or give of the underlying support, the preparation of the canvas, and a host of environmental factors—time of day, temperature, humidity, etc.—all contribute to a procedurally revealing and formally rich variegation. The colored bands transition between areas of pooled-up saturation and sheer translucent washes. Each pass of the squeegee leaves trails of runoff at its edges that register on the surface as gently curving, serpentine lines that run top to bottom. And between these, within the bands themselves, a variety of graceful arabesque shapes appear in the bare patches where the canvas resists the paint altogether. One atop another, these bands are drawn in changing hues and tones, selectively concealing and revealing the under-painting in a way that the artist can anticipate but never wholly control. This, then, is where composition happens, a steadily narrowing window of opportunity: the painting must always be finished before every last trace of the first mark—its origin—is obliterated. This too is a relatively simple formula, on paper at least, but within these given parameters, the variables multiply exponentially.

Works that are "all of one part" are typically planned and then executed in one fell swoop, but the design of Min's multi-part paintings is instead patiently elaborated in the process of making. It takes shape as the accumulated record of a discontinuous series of actions, each responding to the last, while shoring up and rendering visible the interim periods of intellectually detached, sensually focused observation—time spent seated, immobile, taking in what one has already done and planning what to do next. Certainly, this is what all "real" painters do, and it could probably pass unmentioned if the artist did not mention it first and insist on its importance. And this again speaks to the backtracking course of her career path, which lends to the encounter with painterly convention a sense of surprise precisely because she comes at it from an unconventional, perhaps even anti-conventional, perspective.

The work in the studio comes down to somehow calibrating the blind causality of the hand and its aesthetic effect on the eye, a groping in the dark in search of aesthetic illumination. Min's flatbed, tabletop setup and her use of the squeegee and Flasche pigments, which boast an intense, ink-like saturation, is reminiscent of screenprinting, and carries over its inherently incremental unfolding wherein no decision can be wholly erased, covered up or amended. Every gesture is final, and this calls for concerted deliberation on the artist's part at each step in the production process, as well as a corresponding extension of the time lag between these steps. This is not to suggest that there is no room for mistake; rather more accurately one could say that every action attempted under these conditions must be patiently scrutinized as potentially right or wrong. One must "sit with it," sometimes for hours, even days. A successful painting should conform to what the painter would like to see, but it should also exceed expectations as something not yet seen and never before liked. As Theodor Adorno, for one, has noted, the thrill of art making in the most general sense is one of self-alienation, of surrendering some part of oneself to the demands of the material, the tool, the thing. It is not only about the execution of intentions, but the negotiation of intentions, with all the gains and losses this implies. Within this always partly indeterminate equation, an accident may well become a source of revelation, and so must be probed for as yet unimagined potentials. This is true in a general sense, but it is especially true when an artist renounces composing and then resumes it.

In the past, Min selected her colors from a range of mistints at the local paint store. After Duchamp, of course, all color can be considered found, but these are the sorts of colors that proclaim their already made status upfront. Not only are they openly a product of industry—the construction and home improvement industry in this case—but they are chosen by others, and then appropriated. "To make is to choose, and only to choose" goes Duchamp's famous dictum, and here we might add that making is choosing from preexisting choices.[1] However, a key factor of these particular preliminary choices is that they were also rejected; the colors were mixed and then returned to the supplier, and this adds a kind of existential content to the works Min would go on to make with them. As she puts it, what constitutes a "failed color"? And by extension, what constitutes a successful one? Is this merely an arbitrary question of taste, or should taste itself be approached as a concrete social fact, and thereby as something worth exploring on a plane that extends beyond strict formalism? No doubt, a large part of Min's project consisted of redeeming these colors, in making them "work" within an alternate configuration, but without necessarily obscuring their problematic origins.

In addition to its affective and/or ornamental functions, every color is also the color of something—that is, of something else, outside the work. In regard to a painting's referential capacity, color is perhaps the most direct, indexical link between the work and the world. It is what visual art actually shares with external reality, and this is not only because a canvas surface can bear the very same color as the object it represents, but because from the outset the color is not in that object, or even on it, but purely an effect of its appearance. The color is only what we see, and is therefore well-suited to pass between material things and virtual things, like paintings, that exist only to be seen. And yet painting, as the receptacle of colors always transposed from some other thing, inevitably becomes associated with those things. Even when nothing in particular is depicted, the work is nevertheless both metonymically of and metaphorically about whatever else shares its color. In the case of the mistints, this imported content touches on the everyday business of the paint store, on paint as a manufactured product and color as a commodity, on all the various non-art disciplines, such as design and interior decoration, that may have played a part in determining the color of this paint, on the relation between industrial standardization and consumer choice within this professional context, on the aforementioned question of taste and to what extent it is culturally imposed or personally expressed, and so on. Such concerns, already embedded in her pre-mixed paints, were reinforced in their streamlined and modular presentation in color chip-like rows, as well as in the physical interplay of her painted objects within and upon the architectures that they were shown.

In her newer works, those strategies of aesthetic deferral and structural incursion have been emphatically tempered. This turn begins with a palette that does not seem to reflect any predetermined order. Arbitrary to a point that stops just short of signifying arbitrariness, one could almost assume that her palette is freely chosen. And inasmuch as these works are made only of paint—the support structure having been demoted in relevance to a mere convention—this freedom also emerges as a kind of content that cannot be readily traced elsewhere. In a sense, one could say that these paintings are not of or about anything other than what they are in themselves, and yet the career path that led to this point also prepares us to see them differently, not simply as breaks with a former way of working, but a further elaboration on it.

Min has always worked with colored bands. At first they were drawn in straight flag-like rows, one precisely abutting the next, and now they are irregular and overlaying, but the principle remains: The band as an efficient means of relating colors, and by extension, all the things those colors are derived from and stand for. As a template of sorts, it is located somewhere between the color wheel, which we tend to see as a propositional structure imparting a holistic theory of color, and the color grid, which functions conversely to randomize and render any such theory absurd. On the other hand, the colored band speaks to particular interest, to a kind of choosing that aspires to no universal truth, but nevertheless maintains its validity. Here, associations occur within a differential scheme that is openly declared and never transcended. There is no equalization of colors, which stand side-by-side, yet apart. The intervals are emphasized, and even when a color overruns its allotted space and intrudes upon another, it never completely subsumes it; some measure of integrity is always retained. "The color spectrum is continuous," writes Thierry de Duve, "and it is language that cuts it up."[2] What then is the language system operating here? What names shall we give these colors?

For starters, these are not colors we can imagine simply scraping off the "skin of the world," as Maurice Merleau-Ponty would have it, but are rather colors syn-thesized in laboratories by chemists and physicists to brighten the corners of our various artificial paradises: our shopping malls, gyms and spas, amusement parks, clubs and bars. These colors correspond to almost nothing known under the sun. If they maintain any residual connection with nature, it is mainly to that which thrives in obscurity, in the dark of night, deep underground or underwater. Here we find forms of organic and inorganic life that do not selectively reflect the light they are given, but are illuminated from within with the light that they store, like batteries, or secrete from their own cells. Min's paintings operate similarly, for they too appear biolumi-nescent. The predominance of iridescent and fluorescent pigments within her palette points to the somber yet radiant world of gemstones, crystals and pearls, as well as glow worms, fireflies and sub-aquatic fish—a world no longer as exotic and unfamiliar as it once was. Such animal, vegetable and mineral entities that emerge in the absence of sunlight, air and gravity are of course perfectly at home as well on glowing flat-screen monitors, nourished on scrolling codes and data streams. Perhaps this is why they have so consistently served as the aesthetic model of our present environment. This also comprises a content of sorts that comes with her color, for it is stamped with the time signature of the moment and speaks to the conditions of life as they are lived now in spaces contained and secluded, providing maximum physical detachment, yet electronically open and available to all as information. All the delirious exchanges between hiddenness and exposure, proximity and distance that we conduct on an everyday basis are shored up within these colors as well. Together they reflect our contemporary experience of space as a map endlessly folding in upon itself, where everything far comes near and everything near goes far.

Iridescent paints demand intimate inspection; they draw in the eyes to pore over their surface, as their shifting, prismatic effects are literally skin-deep. In this way, they position us and then direct our movements around them, and perhaps most importantly sensitize us to our presence before them. Everything that happens does so because we are there, making it happen. Iridescent paints solicit an active viewership, whereas fluorescent paints assume quite the opposite about us—that we are passive, distracted, remote. These colors were employed early on by the military as a way of marking faraway targets and non-targets, and then in the postwar years by product designers and advertisers to catch the attention of an increasingly restless, mobilized public. This, then, is a projectile color that can be launched across great distances and reliably strike at bodies likewise travelling by at great speed. In Min's paintings, it performs this function as well, an assault on the beholder, and when placed beside a color that conversely retreats and seductively beckons our eyes to follow into its depths, then we are left standing in an impossible place. In the act of composing, she seeks out a point of equilibrium between these opposed forces, as any painter might, but one that remains precarious and thereby always in touch with the no less precarious state of the viewer. Simultaneously expanding and contracting, exploding and imploding, these colors reflect the convulsive relationship we have with an external reality that we have increasingly filled with the stuff of our interior selves. As mentioned, there are rules to their slow accretion, one beside and/or atop another—no cover up or erasure is allowed, and some trace of the origin always remains—but whatever results in the way of procedural record also stubbornly resists a forensic analysis. Rather, it would appear that a painting declares itself done at the point of greatest indeterminacy between what choice came first and what choices followed. David Reed's description of his own works as purposefully confounding is particularly apt in this case, for here too the painting is "a puzzle, not just one that can't be solved but one that shows there are no solutions."[3]

That "there are no solutions" holds as true for the color as for the world that they come from, but in composing these colors, Min also directs them elsewhere. Her embrace of accident in the process of making implicitly argues against that other sort of accident that would only enter the work at the point of conception: the accident of the idea-machine that makes the art, as per Sol LeWitt, and that makes so much else besides. As we know from experience, life itself is most likely to become a continuous succession of those other accidents when it is planned and designed from scratch, or when the idea of what it should be precedes what it actually is. These are the kinds of accidents one can only endure, and if Min's works speak instead to freedom, as suggested earlier, it is because the accidents within them are always negotiable. These paintings allude to a landscape that increasingly conforms to our ideas, the forms of our own inner lives, and that we therefore inhabit much like fish in water, but nevertheless assert the possibility of swimming against the tide.

Notes

1. Marcel Duchamp, from a 1961 interview with Georges Charbonnier, cited in Thierry de Duve, "Echoes of the Readymade: Critique of Pure Modernism," in The Duchamp Effect, eds. Martha Buskirk & Mignon Nixon (Cambridge, MA / London: The MIT Press, 1996), 104.

2. Thierry de Duve, Pictorial Nominalism (Minneapolis, MN: University of Minnesota Press, 1991), 135.

3. David Reed, quoted in Richard Shiff, "Love Her as Herself," David Reed: Leave Yourself Behind, Paintings and Special Projects, 1967-2005 (Wichita, KS: Ulrich Museum of Art, 2005), 39.

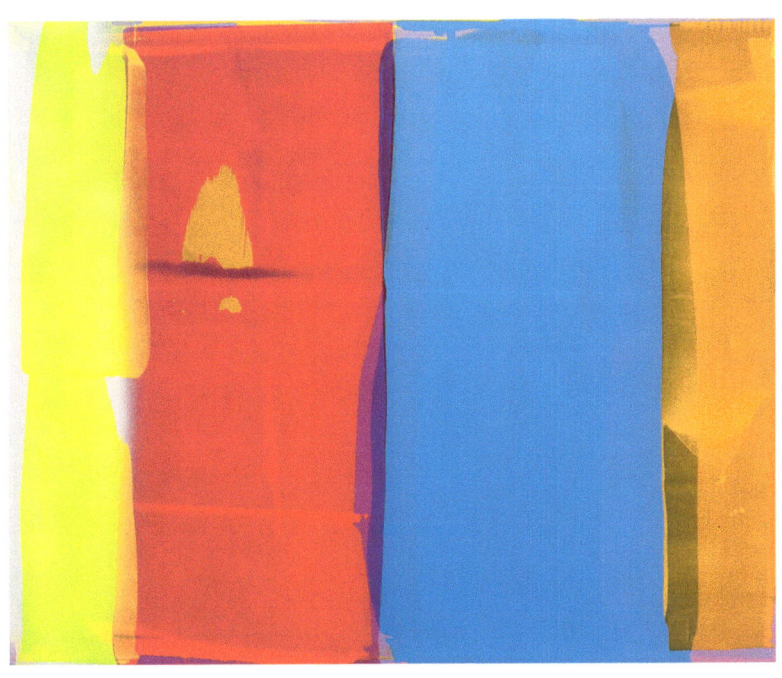

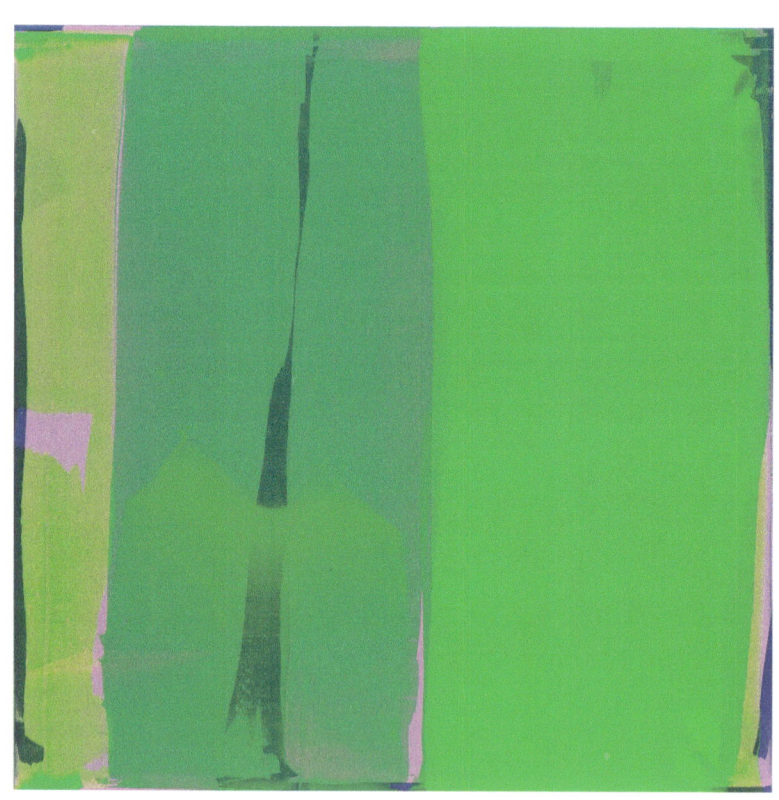

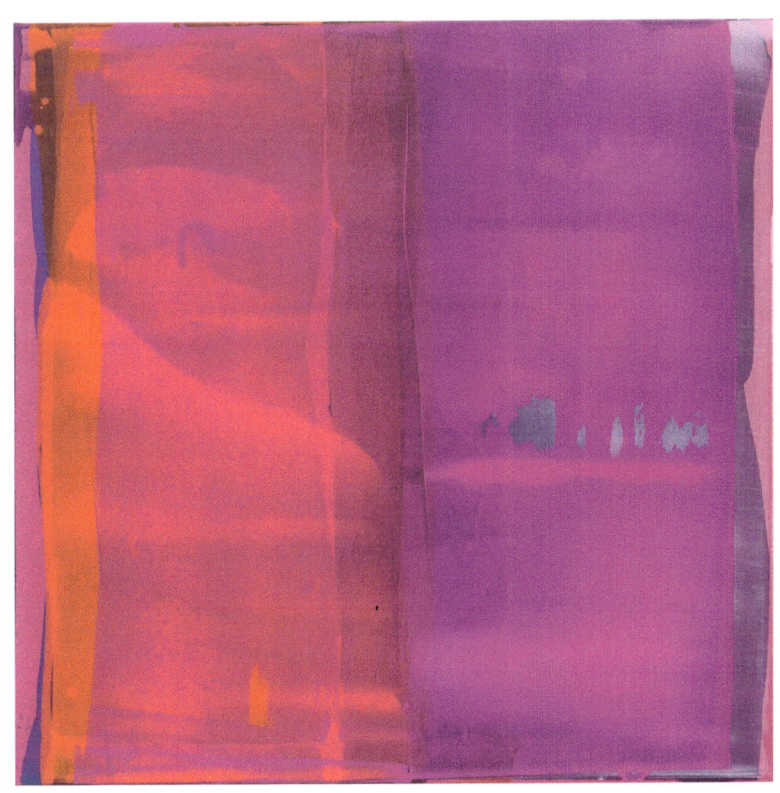

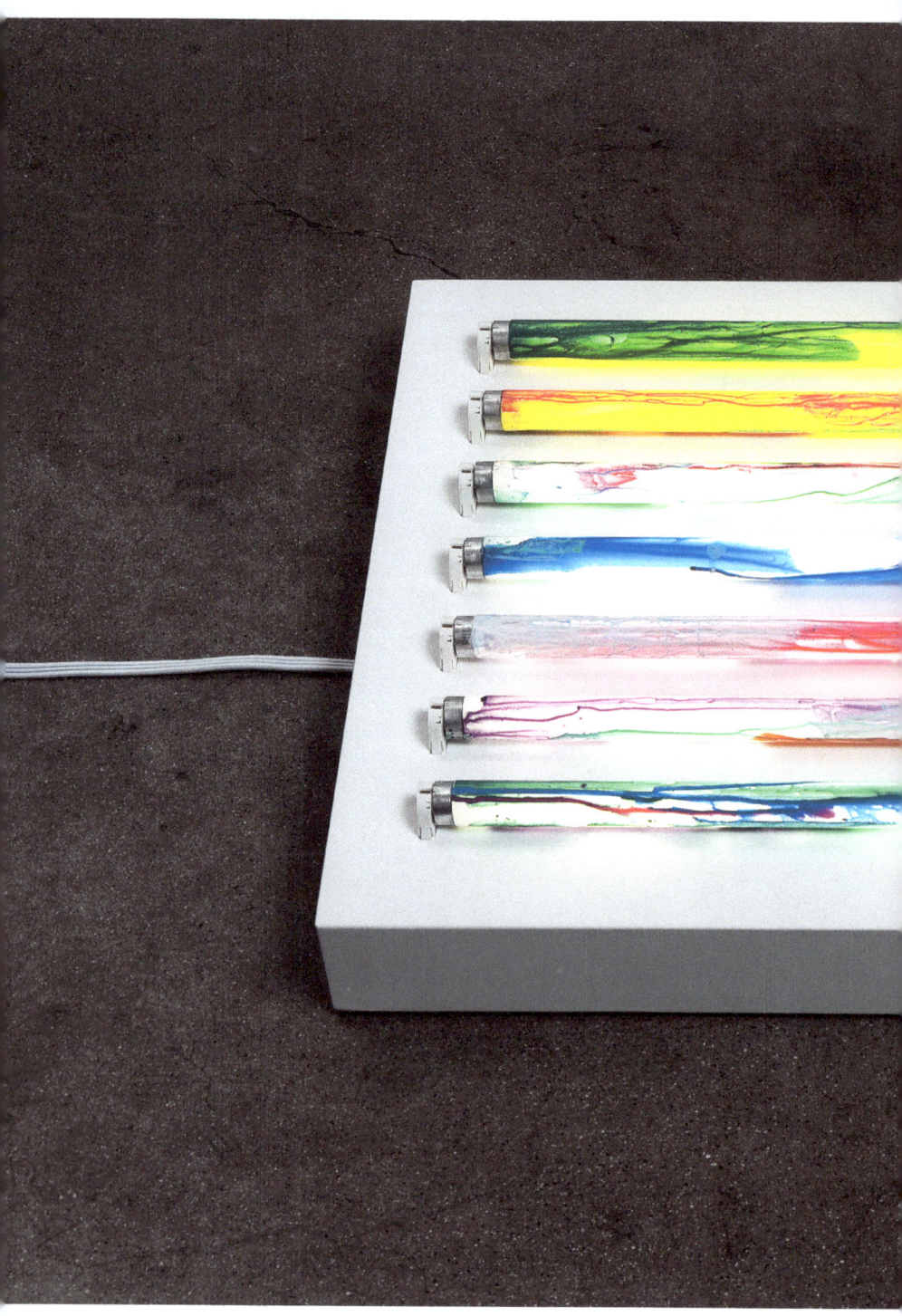

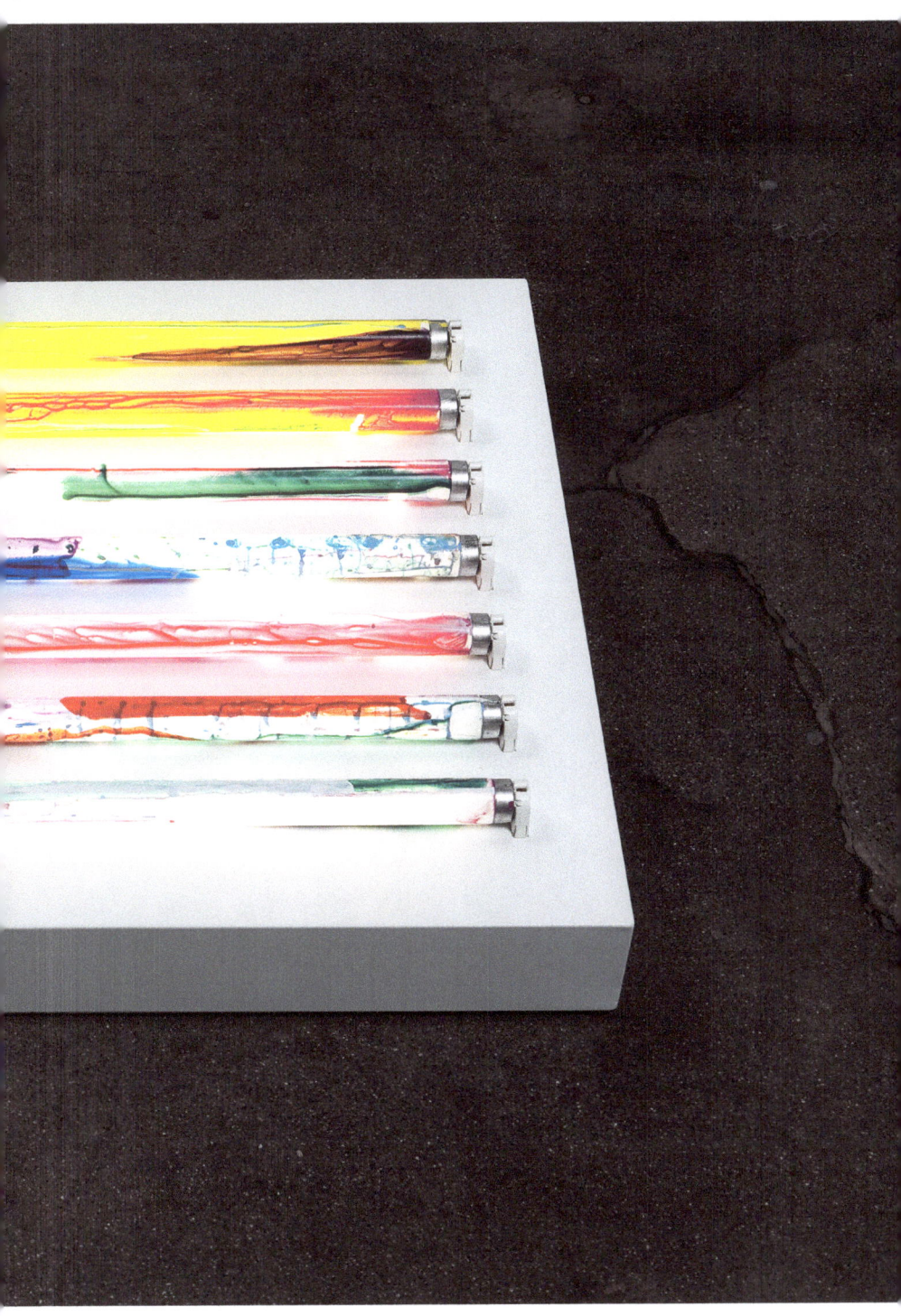

49

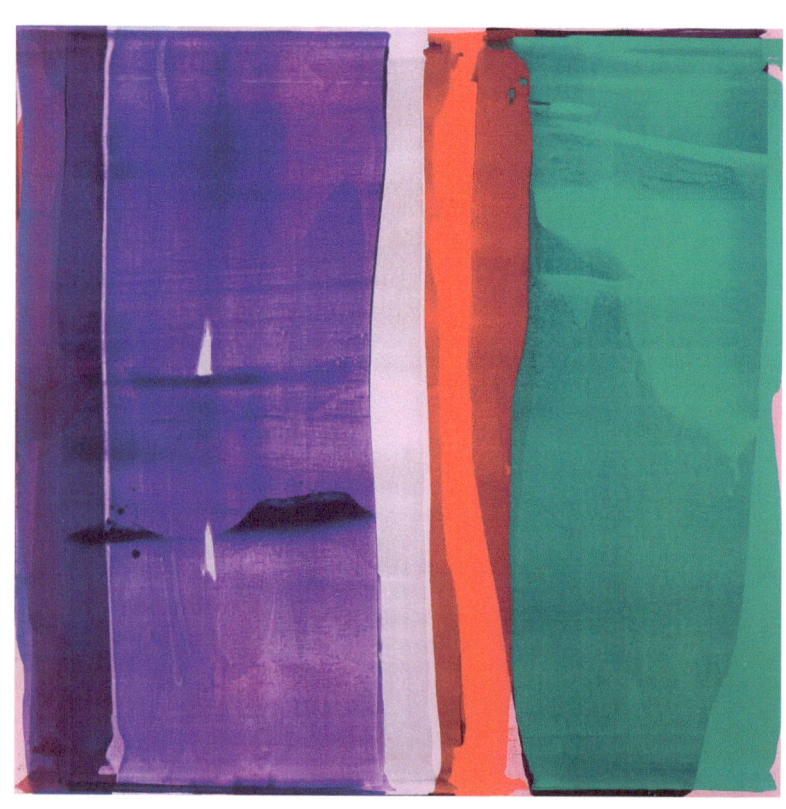

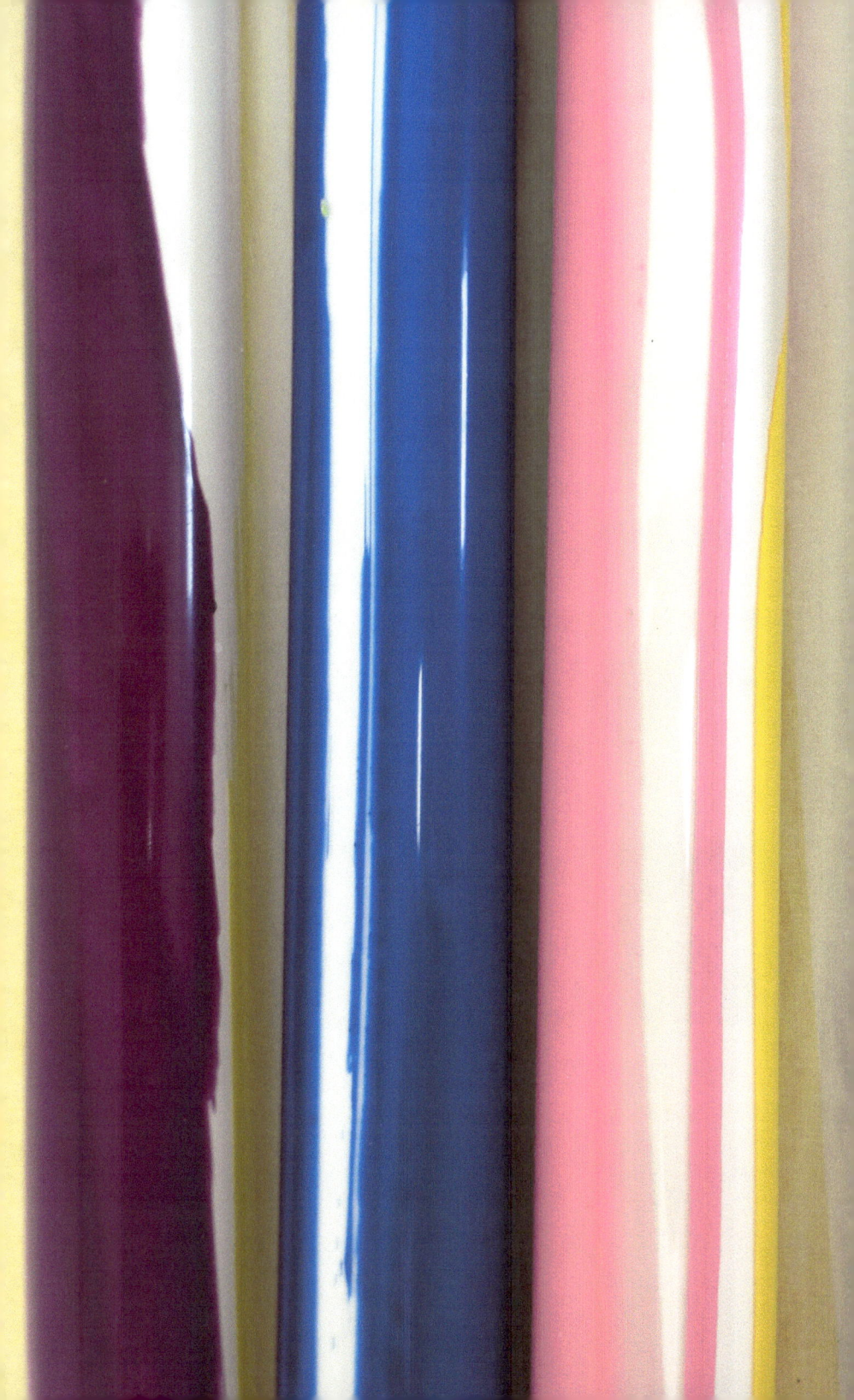

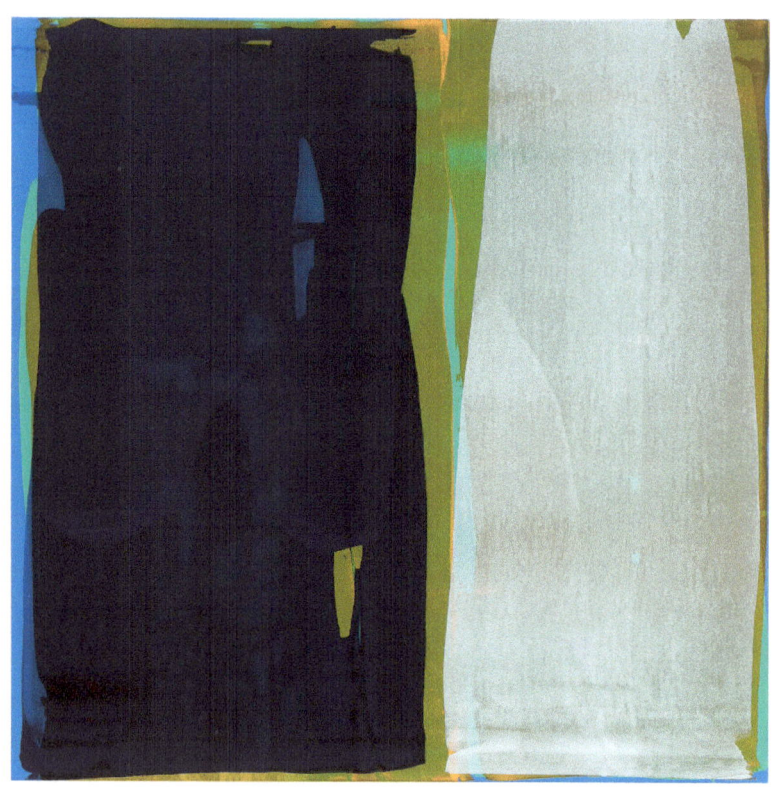

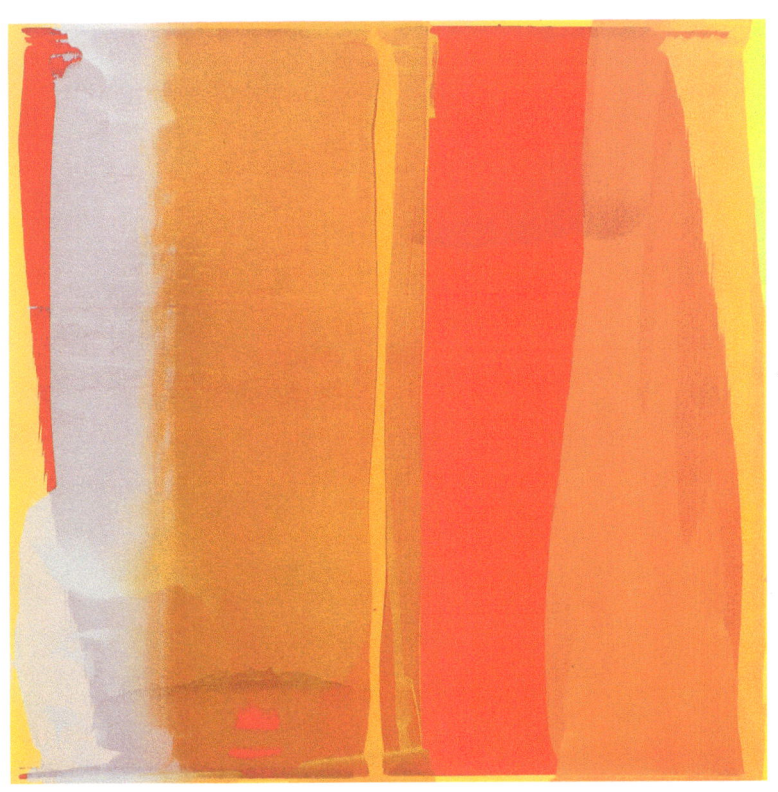

P1. "Into the Sun," Installation view
Susanne Vielmetter LA Projects
June 1 – July 6, 2013

3. "Into the Sun #2," 2013
Acrylic on linen
45" H x 45" W

9. "Summer 5," 2013
Acrylic on canvas
72" H x 84" W

12. "Into the Sun," Installation view
Susanne Vielmetter LA Projects
June 1 – July 6, 2013

15. "Luminaire Delirium (Column #1)," 2013
T8 fluorescent lights, steel, ballasts,
electrical wires and power cord, paint
52.5" H x 12.5" W x 12.5" D

16. "Iridescence + Fluorescence #5," 2013
Acrylic on linen
41" H x 41" W

19. "Iridescence + Fluorescence #6," 2013
Acrylic on linen
41" H x 41" W

20. "Iridescence + Fluorescence #4," 2013
Acrylic on linen
30.75" H x 30.75" W

23. "Into the Sun #1," 2013
Acrylic on linen
60" H x 60" W

24. "Into the Sun #9," 2013
Acrylic on linen
72" H x 84" W

25. "Into the Sun #8," 2013
Acrylic on canvas
72" H x 84" W

26. "Into the Sun," Installation view
Susanne Vielmetter LA Projects
June 1 – July 6, 2013

29. "Into the Sun #3," 2013
Acrylic on linen
40" H x 40" W

41. "Summer 4," 2013
Acrylic on canvas
60" H x 72" W

42. "Tangled up in green," 2014
Acrylic on canvas
45" H x 45" W

43. "Summer 1," 2013
Acrylic on canvas
40" H x 40" W

45. "Summer 7," 2013
Acrylic on canvas
45" H x 45" W

48. "Luminaire Delirium #1," 2013
T8 fluorescent lights, steel, ballasts,
electrical wires, power cord, paint
21" H x 28" W x 5" D

50. "Summer 8," 2013
Acrylic on canvas
60" H x 60" W

52. "Two moons," 2014
Acrylic on canvas
45" H x 45" W

53. "Into the Sun #5," 2013
Acrylic on canvas
60" H x 60" W

58. "Summer 2," 2013
Acrylic on canvas
45" H x 45" W

YUNHEE MIN

Born in Seoul, Korea
Lives and works in Los Angeles

EDUCATION

2007   MA, Harvard University, Graduate School of Design, Cambridge, MA
1994   Kunstakademie, Düsseldorf, Germany
1991   BFA, Art Center College of Design, Pasadena, CA

SOLO EXHIBITIONS & PROJECTS

2013   "Into the Sun," Susanne Vielmetter Los Angeles Projects, Culver City, CA
        "NG2," Window installation, Inaugural exhibition, Night Gallery, Los Angeles, CA
2012   "For Instance," Installation at the Lindbrook Terrace, Hammer Museum, Los
            Angeles, CA
        "Spectra: fixtures, attachments, and ornamentals," Exercise, Vancouver, BC
2011   "Rise," Independent Art Fair, New York, NY
        "Collective Show Los Angeles 2011," Silvershed, Los Angeles, CA
2010   "Attraction," Susanne Vielmetter Los Angeles Projects, Culver City, CA
2009   "Continuum: Structure #003," LAXART, Los Angeles, CA
        "Fly like a Butterfly, Sting Like a Bee," guest curator, Artist Curated Projects, Los
            Angeles, CA
2008   "Recent paintings," James Harris Gallery, Seattle, WA
        "For Instance," The Graduate Center at the City University of New York, The Amioe and
            Tony James Gallery, New York, NY
2006   "Above & Beyond (x, y, z)," Pasadena Museum of Contemporary Art, Pasadena, CA
2005   "'Distance is Like the Future,' Circa Series: Yunhee Min," Museum of Contemporary Art
            San Diego, San Diego, CA
        "another country," Susanne Vielmetter Los Angeles Projects, Culver City, CA
        "iT House, OutFiT" Design for Taalman Koch Architecture, Los Angeles, CA
2004   "Fading Wild," Finesilver Gallery, San Antonio, TX
        "Double Positive," ArtPace, San Antonio, TX
2003   James Harris Gallery, Seattle, WA
        "Out of bounds, from near and afar," Yerba Buena Center for the Arts, San
            Francisco, CA
        "Corrugate," Susanne Vielmetter Los Angeles Projects, Los Angeles, CA
2002   Luckman Gallery, California State University, Los Angeles, CA
2001   James Harris Gallery, Seattle, WA
2000   ACME, Los Angeles, CA

GROUP EXHIBITIONS

2013   "Spectra," San Diego State University Downtown Gallery, San Diego, CA
        "Nacker Gläubigen," curated by Davida Nemeroff, Infernoesque//Pascal Richter, Berlin
        "The Object Salon," curated by Calvin Marcus, Roberts & Tilton Gallery, Los Angeles,
            CA
2012   "Lost Line: Contemporary Art From the Collection," Los Angeles County Museum of Art,
            Los Angeles, CA
        "Vis-á-vis Visitation Field," collaboration with Patrick Meagher, curated by Aaron
            Wrinkle, Cirrus Gallery, Los Angeles, CA
2011   "Plain Brown Wrapper," curated by Molly Larkey, Human Resources, Los Angeles, CA
        "Painting in Parts," curated by Michael Klein, Maryland Art Place, Baltimore, MD
2010   "WP9," Yunhee Min, Patrick Meagher, Miles Coolidge, Night Gallery, Los Angeles, CA
2008   "Claire Cowie: 12 Views || Yunhee Min: New Paintings," James Harris Gallery,
            Seattle, WA
        "Digital With Monument," The Silvershed, New York, NY
2007   "Merit Badge 2," curated by Jason Middlebrook, Rockland Center for the Arts,
            West Nyack, NY
2006   "Too Much Love," curated by Amy Adler, Angles Gallery, Los Angeles, CA
        "The Trans-Aestheticization of Daily Life," Sweeney Art Gallery, Riverside, CA

2005	"Wall Painting," curated by Frances Colpitt, UTSA Art Gallery at the University of Texas at San Antonio, San Antonio, TX
	"Around About Abstraction," Weatherspoon Museum, Greensboro, NC
	"20 scene 05," Korean American Museum, Los Angeles, CA
2004	"New," Susanne Vielmetter Los Angeles Projects, Inaugural exhibition of Culver City space, Culver City, CA
	"Yunhee Min - Herbert Hamak," ArtSource, San Francisco, CA
2003	"Warped Space," curated by Ralph Rugoff, CCA Wattis Institute for Contemporary Arts, San Francisco, CA
	"International Abstraction: Making Painting Real," curated by Lisa Corrin, Seattle Art Museum, Seattle, WA
	"Abstraction," curated by Eungie Joo, Artists Space, New York, NY
2001	"Cal's Art," University of North Texas Art Gallery, Denton, TX
	"Rogue Wave," LA Louver Gallery, Venice, CA
	"Snapshot: New Art from Los Angeles," Hammer Museum, Los Angeles, CA; traveled to Museum of Contemporary Art North Miami, Miami, FL
	"Curious," Altoids Collection, New Museum, New York, NY
2000	"The Next Wave," curated by Norkio Gamblin, California Center for the Arts, Escondido, CA
	"KOREAMERICAKOREA," curated by David Ross and Sun-Jung Kim, Sonje Museum of Contemporary Art, Seoul, South Korea; traveled to Gyeongju, South Korea
	"Deterritorialization of Process," curated by Michael Joo, Artists Space, New York, NY
	"Shimmer," curated by Thomas Lawson, Municipal Art Gallery, Barnsdall Art Park, Los Angeles, CA
1999	"Hubcap Diamond Star Halo," curated by Leonardo Bravo and Christopher Miles, Peggy Phelps Gallery, Claremont Graduate University, Claremont, CA
	"Other Paintings," curated by Julie Joyce, Huntington Beach Art Center, Huntington Beach, CA
	"Structural elements," Views of Architecture and Architectural Elements, Transamerica Pyramid Lobby, San Francisco, CA
	"Under 500/Intimate Abstract Painting," curated by James Hayward, Black Dragon Society, Los Angeles, CA
	"After the Gold rush," curated by Joe Wallin and Lia Gangitano, Thread Waxing Space, New York, NY

GRANTS, AWARDS, AND RESIDENCIES

2013	Storefront for Art and Architecture, New York, NY (Silvershed and Zellenerplus)
2010	Aurobora Press, San Francisco, CA
2009	Artist in Residence, Jeju Museum of Contemporary Art, Jeju-Do, South Korea
2006	Alpert Ucross Residency Prize, Clearmont, WY
2003	Wattis Artist in Residence, Yerba Buena Center for the Arts, San Francisco, CA
1999	City of Los Angeles Cultural Affairs Individual Artist Grant, Los Angeles, CA

PUBLIC COLLECTIONS

Hammer Museum, Los Angeles, CA
Los Angeles County Museum of Art, Los Angeles, CA
Museum of Contemporary Art San Diego, San Diego, CA
Nerwin Museum, Kansas City, MO
New Museum, New York, NY

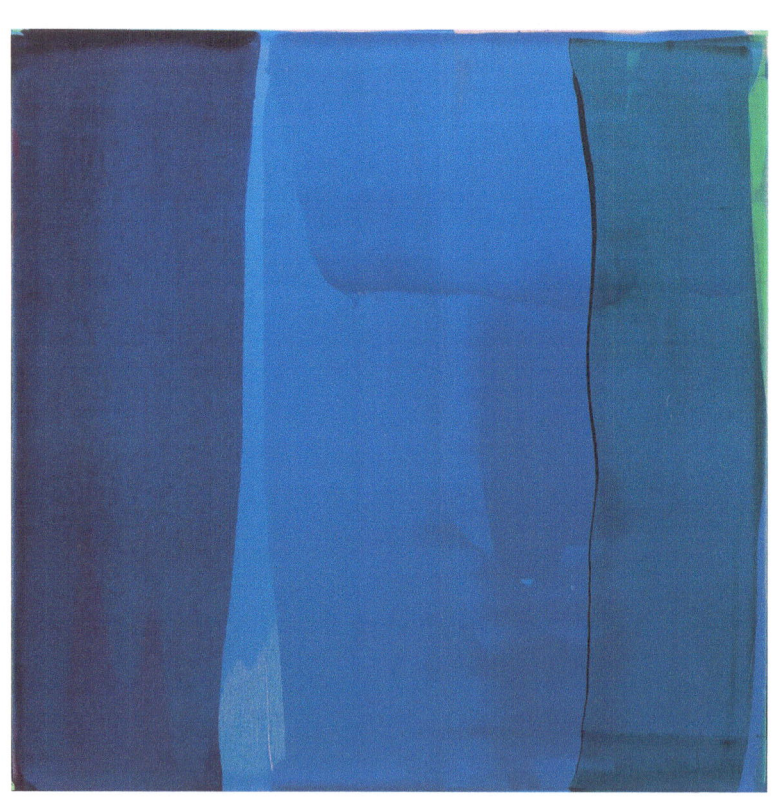

YUNHEE MIN
ISBN: 978-0-9911092-5-8
Essays: Daniel Mendel-Black, Jan Tumlir
Layout and Design: Paul Soto, Susanne Vielmetter
Printing: Insert Blanc Press, Los Angeles
All images courtesy of Susanne Vielmetter Los Angeles Projects

www.ingramcontent.com/pod-product-compliance
Lightning Source LLC
Chambersburg PA
CBHW052059170526
45162CB00006BA/50